GREAT ASCENTS

David & Charles

Newton Abbot · London · Vancouver

Eric Newby

GREAT ASCENTS

A Narrative History of Mountaineering

ISBN 0 7153 7408 7

Set in 10 on 12 Goudy Old Style
by Ronset Ltd., Darwen, Lancs.
and printed in Great Britain
by The Alden Press, Oxford
for David & Charles
(Publishers) Limited
Brunel House   Newton Abbot
Devon

Published in Canada
by Douglas David & Charles Ltd.
1875 Welch Street
North Vancouver   BC

To Wanda, who kept me going

CONTENTS

INTRODUCTION

When I began to write this book, beginning at the beginning of climbing, I soon realised that the problem was not going to be deciding what to include, but what to leave out. I found myself in the same dilemma as a man in a saloon who wonders whether he will live long enough to have a shot from all the bottles.

It certainly meant excluding anyone who climbed mountains for any more tangible reason than getting to the top, which I take to be the true, loony test of a mountaineer, even though he may disguise his intentions by announcing that he is only going to check the height—like Dr Paccard, the first man to reach the summit of Mont Blanc.

It meant leaving out Noah, the shipwrecked sailor with an embarrassing cargo, an involuntary man of the mountains—one of the few to descend from a detached peak without having climbed it. It meant saying goodbye to Abraham, preparing to carve up Isaac on Mount Moriah (enough to put one off climbing with one's father); and to Moses on that draughty mountain, Sinai, at least I found it so, being nearly blown off it one winter; and to Hannibal crossing the Cottian Alps. It meant ignoring Cortes' soldiers in search of sulphur to make gunpowder in the crater at the summit of Popocatépetl, with which to exterminate the Aztecs. From here, at a height of nearly 18,000ft, they could look down on their fabulous capital, Tenochtitlan, which lay as if floating in a great lagoon. Even more regretfully I steeled myself to leave out those Andean Indians who, around the fourteenth century, left a mummified body in sacrificial robes on the 6,380m Cerro de Toro on the borders of Argentine and Chile; and the sadhus, semi-naked on the ice at the source of the Ganges, 12,700ft up in the Kumaun Himalaya. In our own time I even had to leave out the young Foreign Service secretaries who used to, and may still for all I know, pound up the, perhaps 1,000ft high, Legation Hill above the British Embassy at Kabul, before breakfast—because they only did it to cure a hangover. In fact, having written about them, I was forced to leave out the accounts of great ascents in Britain entirely, on the grounds that the book would have become intolerably long. They will have to wait for another time. Perhaps it is all for the best. So many of the pioneering climbs in all parts of the world were made by British climbers that readers of other nationalities might be pardoned for finding their ubiquity slightly monotonous.

I hesitate to even hazard a guess as to why other men and women climb. 'Because it is there', Mallory's dictum, always seemed rather barren and slightly brittle in the idiom of Coward: 'Did you like the Himalayas? Liked him, hated her.'

My own feelings, engendered in the course of a spectacularly short high-climbing career, about the reasons for doing it, are to some extent summed up by the unaggressive Professor Konrad Gesner of Zürich, writing to a friend at Glarus in 1543, when he was twenty-seven.

I have resolved for the future, so long as God suffers me to live, to climb, or at all events to climb one mountain every year . . . partly for the sake of studying botany, and partly for the delight of the mind and the proper exercise of the body. For what, think you, is the pleasure, what the joy affected as it should be, to marvel at the spectacle of the mighty masses of the mountains, and lift up one's head, as it were, among the clouds.

A far cry from the view of the hard men fighting their way up the Eigerwand above the embrasure on the Jungfrau Railway, or putting in the Rurps (Realised Ultimate Reality Pitons) on some big limestone wall in the Yosemite Valley; or half-way up the Old Man of Hoy, being given the treatment by the Orkney sea-birds—not worse, just different.

By my own, self-established rules I *would* have included in the main text had I not given them mention here: Philip of Macedon who climbed Mount Haemus in the Balkans in order to find if he could see the Adriatic and the Aegean at the same time; the Emperor Hadrian who ascended Mount Etna to see the sun rise; Empedocles who may have followed his sandals into the self-same crater; Petrarch who climbed Mont Ventoux in the Vaucluse, another windy mountain, and Leonardo da Vinci, climbing on what may have been Monte Viso, near what was very probably Hannibal's crossing place, perhaps transmuting, in his artistic imagination, the rocks, much as any others in the Cottian Alps, into the wonderful, haunting structures we see in the background of many of his paintings and drawings.

Apart from Petrarch's effort there is not much more to be said about these climbs, apart from recording them. More is known about a rather nasty climb which Dompjulien de Beaupré, Capitaine de Montélimar, Chamberlain to Charles VIII of France, was *ordered* to carry out, in 1492, on Mont Aiguille (6,880ft), an astonishing limestone reef, rather like a domino on edge, to the east of the great Plateau de Vercors, south of Grenoble—because the King, while on pilgrimage, had heard stories from the local inhabitants, who may have known a sucker when they saw one, of angels' tunics having been seen floating over the escarpments.

'After the most horrible and frightful passage that I or any of my company have ever seen, you have to ascend half a league by ladder, and a league by other ways'—one of the King's laddermen employed 'subtle means and engines'—they found themselves in a beautiful green meadow where, although there were no angels *en déshabille*, there was a fine herd of chamois. It was not climbed again until 1834 and as late as 1902, the author of Baedeker's *Southern France* was able to write that 'the ascent takes two and a half hours from the foot of the cliffs and is fit only for steady heads and sure-footed mountaineers; a rope and a guide (20fr.) are necessary. The view is rather limited.'

What sympathy and admiration one has for the involuntary climbers—those who never intended to climb at all. Men such as Shackleton, the great Antarctic explorer, crossing the unexplored mountains and glaciers of South Georgia with a small party, none of whom had any previous climbing experience. And this after a nightmare 800-mile journey in a 20ft open boat through the Scotia Sea, one of the stormiest seas in the world, in order to seek help for the rest of the shipwrecked expedition awaiting rescue on Elephant Island. It was one of the most brilliantly executed and courageous combined operations of all time.

What courage was displayed by the willing but completely amateur climbers, some of them dotty or half dotty, many of whom were, and still are, disapproved of by 'real' climbers or, if they did what they set out to do and survived, were often disbelieved. Scarcely anyone believed the gold prospectors, the Sourdoughs, when they returned from the first successful climb of the 20,320ft Mount McKinley in Alaska—because, at that time, it was rare for anyone who was not more or less a gentleman, (apart from guides who were presumed to be natural gentlemen, and very often were) to climb mountains. Far fewer

Americans questioned Dr Cook's claim to have reached the top, which he substantiated with forgery, although he was never anywhere near it. One should not even be sorry for, let alone disapprove of, the more than eccentric Englishman, Maurice Wilson, who having never climbed before was found dead at Camp 3 below the North Col, 21,000ft up Everest, having attempted the mountain alone on a diet of rice water. It was his own choice and at least no one died in an attempt to save him. The Dane, Klause Becker-Larsen, was luckier. He crossed the 19,000ft Nangpa La between Nepal and Tibet, westwards of Cho Oyu, probably the highest trading pass in the world, and, in spite of the Chinese presence, reached the Rongbuk Monastery on the north side of Everest and returned to tell the tale.

There was also, in a slightly different category because she was not alone, one who was perhaps the uncrowned queen of successful amateurs. The American schoolmistress, Miss Annie Peck, did not even begin her career as a mountaineer until she was forty-seven, when she tackled the Matterhorn, and, at the age of fifty-eight on a second attempt in appallingly cold weather, reached the unclimbed, 21,834ft North Summit of Huascaran in the Cordillera Blanca of Peru, together with two guides from Zermatt. Another woman of similar mettle, although scarcely amateur in the true sense, was Gertrude Bell, explorer, archaeologist and friend of T. E. Lawrence. In 1902 she was one of a party who made a protracted attack on the unclimbed North-East Face of the Finsteraarhorn in the Bernese Oberland, forty-eight hours of which were spent roped on it, immobilised by a blizzard. It was of Miss Bell, by no means Amazonian in appearance, that an Arab chief is said to have remarked, 'And this is one of their women! Allah, what must their men be like?' I only wish I could discover more about two amazing Scottish pioneers, Mrs and Miss Campbell, mother and daughter, who as early as 1822, succeeded in making the hazardous crossing of the Col du Géant (11,000ft) between France and Italy in the Mont Blanc massif.

It is difficult to capture the world inhabited by mountaineers in its various aspects because so much of it is hidden and partly forgotten, embalmed in dusty volumes, many of them produced with an amplitude that would be impossible to-day, which no one ever appears to move, all standing in the dimly-lit transepts of great libraries, often under SCIENCE: Mountaineering; but they are there, if anyone cares to dig, and reading them you experience all the emotions that man can experience under stress—the vast loneliness of Norton on Everest in 1924, wearing a trilby hat of a sort men wore to go to a country race-meeting at that time. He stood there alone, without oxygen, at the highest point attained by man at that time—28,126ft beyond the Great Couloir, only 80ft lower than the summit of Kangchenjunga, the third highest mountain of the world. Smythe, also alone and also unbelayed, the greatest test of fortitude such a mountain can provide, was in more or less the same position nine years later, on a ledge covered with new snow, 'soft like flour and loose like caster sugar. Imagine a house-roof covered with loose snow of such consistency that it cannot hold the foot and thus prevent a slip,' he wrote. A 9,000ft sheer drop below him was the Rongbuk Glacier. And there is Buhl, who reached the summit of the terrible Nanga Parbat alone, in 1953, and then, on the descent, benighted at 26,000ft, he stood, leaning against a rock for hours, waiting for the moon to rise—the highest, solitary bivouac ever made until that time. By 1954 the only two other men who had survived a night in the open at such an altitude and lived were Walter Bonatti and Mahdi, a Pakistani porter, on the successful Italian attempt on K2, and they were about 200ft higher. All of them were short of the 28,000ft bivouac on the South-East Ridge of Everest, made by the Americans in 1963 which resulted—and they were lucky it was a calm night— in one man losing all his toes and the tops of his little fingers, another all his toes except one. 'They paid a stiff price for standing, each for his few minutes, on the summit of Everest', wrote James Ramsay Ullman who was on the expedition. 'Was it worth it?. The final answer must be their own.'

It is all there to be excavated, the splendours and the miseries, the splendours exemplified by Filippo de Filippi's description of K2 in the Karakoram, as he saw it for the first time on the Duke of Abruzzi's expedition of 1909.

> Suddenly, and without warning, as if a veil had been lifted from our eyes, the wide Godwin-Austen valley lay before us in its whole length. Down at the end, alone, detached from all the other mountains, soared up K2, the indisputable sovereign of the region, gigantic and solitary, hidden from human sight by innumerable ranges, jealously defended by a vast throng of vassal peaks, protected from invasion by miles and miles of glaciers.

And there is Whymper's description of a storm at the third platform on the Italian Ridge of the Matterhorn, six men wedged in a five-man tent at 12,992ft which is enough to make any climber's hair stand on end:

> Forked lightning shot out at the turrets above, and at the crags below. It was so close that we quailed at its darts. It seemed to scorch us, we were in the very focus of the storm. The thunder was simultaneous with the flashes; short and sharp, and more like the noise of a door that is violently slammed, multiplied a thousand-fold, than any noise to which I can compare it.

And there are the great horrors and tragedies: the Matterhorn disaster, the death of Mummery and his faithful Gurkhas on Nanga Parbat; but worse than these are the long, drawn out agonies: Kurz, the length of an ice-axe from his rescuers on the Eigerwand, one arm frozen solid after a night in a sling on the face, then swinging away with the words 'I'm finished.'; the death march from Camp 8 on Nanga Parbat in 1934, with the fine flower of the Sherpas and the climbers dying one by one; the horror of the retreat from Annapurna. Is it worth it? It must be worth it; but neither words nor photographs can really convey to those who have not seen them the awesomeness of such walls as the South Face of Annapurna, the Rupal Flank (14,900ft) of Nanga Parbat, one of the world's great mural precipices, or the scale of Everest.

Yet it is not only height which is impressive, but exposure. This is what Don Whillans, one of the first men to climb the South Face of Annapurna, and Joe Brown, who later made the first ascent of Kangchenjunga, with George Band, had to say about the Cemetery Gates on Dinas Cromlech in Snowdonia: 'It looked like a hell of a route to me,' Whillans wrote.

> I hung on to slings attached to poor spikes sticking out of the rock a few feet higher [Brown wrote]. 'This was the first stance in slings as it is called. . . . The position on the face was very sensational and frightening [Whillans, a real tough egg, called it 'scary' in his autobiography] I brought up Don [Whillans led the second pitch] and he was flabbergasted. 'Christ this is a gripping place'.

Yet they were only 70ft above the foot of the cliff.

And as we advance beyond free climbing, into a world of dynamic belays and tension climbing, as carried out on the great spires and faces of Yosemite and in South California, a new kind of climbing evolves which has its own beauty for its followers, with men like the great Swiss wrought-iron worker Salathé forging pitons for the Yosemite walls, using the rear axle of a Model A Ford for prototypes which are now collectors' items; or Yvon Chouinard, another great ironmonger, who turned the back of an old truck into a forge, literally on site, below Kat pinnacle, the most difficult climb in America, which he climbed with Frost, using the first Rurps (realised ultimate reality pitons), the thickness of a knife blade, which only needed to penetrate ¼in into the rock to hold.

Perhaps this book should have been called 'Great Ascents and Great Attempts'—for the ascent is not the whole story. What about those who tried and discovered the way? The Chinese without the British to show them the way on the Tibetan side of Everest; the British without the Swiss pioneers in Nepal on the Geneva Spur which gave them the key to the South Col—the Swiss themselves without earlier reconnaissances by others. And where would any of them been without the devoted services of their porters and the Alpine guides, especially the early ones, companies which both deserve to occupy a well heated hall in the mountaineer's Valhalla.

MONT BLANC
AND THE EARLY DAYS
IN THE ALPS

1 Before the Climbers Came

What first drew the attention, at least that of the fashionable world, to Chamonix and its glaciers and peaks was the unannounced arrival there, on 21 June 1741, of a party of eight gentlemen, all members of the British Colony at Geneva, whose presence in this remote Alpine village must have caused a considerable stir among the local inhabitants.

Among the party was Richard Pococke, a thirty-seven year old clergyman, who later became an Irish bishop. To the end of his life an indefatigable traveller, he was on his way home from a journey of almost four years' duration, in the course of which he visited Egypt (travelling up the Nile), Palestine (bathing in the Dead Sea), Syria (visiting Baalbek), Turkey (acquiring an Oriental costume in which he posed for an excellent full-length portrait), Cyprus, Greece and Crete (climbed Mount Ida, otherwise Idhi Oros, 2,456m, now a difficult six-hour walk for non-mountaineers).

Another member of the party was William Windham of Felbrigg in Norfolk, an athletic and wealthy young man of twenty-four, also known as 'Boxing Windham'. Later, he became an officer in a regiment of Hungarian hussars. Rows with his father caused him to live abroad and he had spent four years in France, Italy and Switzerland. And there was Benjamin Stillingfleet, grandson of the Bishop of Worcester, a naturalist and dilettante, Windham's companion and one-time tutor. It was he who helped Windham to write the account of the expedition. They took with them five servants, all of them armed, and Windham, when he wrote his short account of the expedition, recommended any subsequent travellers to Chamonix to

be armed, 'One is never the worse for it and oftentimes it helps a Man out of a Scrape.'

It took them three days, travelling with riding and baggage-horses, to reach Chamonix from Geneva. They camped in meadows—they had a tent with them—and also slept in barns on the way. The route was wild and wonderful; and from the village of Chamonix, still basking in anonymity as far as the rest of the world was concerned, they had their first view of the *Glacières:*

These appeared [Windham wrote] only like white Rocks, or rather like immense Icicles made by water running down the Mountain. This did not satisfy our curiosity, and we thought we were coming too far to be contented with so small a Matter; we therefore strictly inquired of the Peasants whether we could not by going up the Mountain itself discover something more worth our Notice.

None of the locals were enthusiastic for a sightseeing trip, except on their own terms. The only reason that any of them ever visited the mountains was in pursuit of *bouquetins* (ibex) and chamois, or in search of crystal. According to them '. . . all the Travellers, who had been to the *Glacières* hitherto, had been satisfied with what we had already seen.'

How well one can visualise the scene. The little party of Englishmen, all of whom had probably left their wigs at Geneva, all used to having their own way, now strengthened in their resolve to overcome the obstacles put in their path by peasantry in whom gormlessness and craftiness, generosity and venality were bewilderingly compounded. It was the

Richard Pococke, clergyman, indefatigable traveller and early Alpinist, wearing the Oriental costume he acquired on his travels. Portrait by Liotard (*Musée d'Art et d'Histoire, Geneva*)

Chamonix, below Mont Blanc, in the first half of the nineteenth century (*RGS*)

classic situation in which English travellers abroad would continue to find themselves far into the twentieth century.

'We determined to climb the Mountain', Windham wrote, and of course they did. In this case the 'Mountain' was the Montanvert (now the Montenvers) on the west side of the Mer de Glace, since 1908 reached by a rack-and-pinion railway. They set off about noon and climbed up among larch and fir trees, making frequent halts, which was pretty sensible, and refreshing themselves with wine mixed with spring water.

It took them four and three-quarter hours to reach the summit (it now takes two to two and a half by a made path), and at some points they had to cross the paths of ava-lanches of the previous winter, where trees had been torn out by the roots and the ground underfoot was a disagreeable mixture of mud and snow, 'and had it not been for our Staffs [these were iron-shod poles about 8ft long, used by the inhabitants for crossing crevasses] and our Hands, we must many

times have gone down to the Bottom of the Mountain, and the Steepness of the Descent, join'd to the Height where we were, made a View terrible enough to make most People's Heads turn.'

From the summit, where there was a shepherd's hut they had a splendid view of the Mer de Glace and of the surrounding peaks, although these are not specified. Closest to them would have been the great pinnacle of the Aiguille du Dru (3,754m), an enormous granite obelisk, first climbed in 1878, with the Aiguille Verte (4,122m), looming behind it. Far away, at the head of the glacier they would have seen the great ice and rock face of the Grandes Jorasses and to the right the Aiguille des Grands Charmoz (3,444m), first climbed by a French party in 1885, one of the now world-famous Chamonix Aiguilles.

Of the Mer de Glace, Windham wrote: 'The Description which Travellers give of the Seas of *Greenland* seem to come nearest to it. You must imagine your Lake put in

14

Mont Blanc and the Chamonix
Aiguilles (*John Cleare*)

Agitation by a strong Wind frozen all at once, perhaps even that would not produce the same Appearance.'

Naturally, nothing would content the gentlemen but that they should go down on the glacier itself, which they did, by slithering about 120m or so down the lateral moraine.

In spite of the interest aroused by such early visits, few travellers, and the majority of these British, visited Chamonix until, in 1760, a distinguished young Genevese professor, named Horace Bénédict de Saussure, offered a reward to the first man to reach the summit of Mont Blanc. At about this time, too, a writer named Bourrit began to write about the region. During the summer months he lived in a chalet at Chamonix, where he prepared itineraries for visitors and acted as a sort of travel-agent. In 1775 the first serious attempt to climb the mountain was made, the first of a series of gallant expeditions which finally culminated in the summit being reached in 1786.

2 Victory Approaches

When Dr Michel-Gabriel Paccard and the guide Jacques Balmat succeeded in reaching the summit of Mont Blanc, the highest mountain in Western Europe, on 8 August 1786, the impression which the news of their climb made on the comparatively few people who heard it at the time was rather similar to that which the news of the first landing on the moon made on a far wider audience in July 1969, although this was not the first ascent of a high Alpine mountain.

As early as 1778, Jean Joseph Beck, a domestic servant from Gressoney, led a large party to the top of the Lysjoch (4,153m), while searching for a hidden valley—a height record not surpassed until Mont Blanc was climbed.

The Mont Blanc Range itself is situated on the borders of France, Italy and Switzerland. It is about 40km long from south west to north east and covers an area of 645 square kilometres, approximately 160 square kilometres being covered by glaciers. The largest of these glaciers, and the fourth longest in the Alps, the Mer de Glace, covers an area of 52 square kilometres. Within the range there are twenty-five mountain tops more than 4,000m high.

The main peak of the massif, the summit of Mont Blanc, is 4,807m high. The peak itself lies entirely in France, but a lesser summit is situated on the Italian side of the frontier, and is linked to it by a short ridge. This is Mont Blanc de Courmayeur, 4,748m, which takes its name from the village of Courmayeur, some 3,500m below in Italy.

The northern side of the mountain, on French territory, was to be the battlefield on which early attempts to reach the summit

would be fought out. The approaches on the southern, Italian, side are far more labyrinthine, consisting of a number of glacier basins separated by high and difficult ridges.

Interest in climbing Mont Blanc was stimulated by the activities of Professor de Saussure who first became attracted by the possibility of climbing Mont Blanc in 1760, in which year he offered a generous reward to anyone who could find a way to the summit which he might follow in order to make scientific observations.

Between 1760 and 1789 he made extensive journeys through the Alpine regions, climbing various peaks, visiting glaciers, carrying out scientific experiments and making observations. In 1767 he made the first circumambulation of Mont Blanc, now a popular, six-day excursion known as Le Tour de Mont Blanc. In 1789 he became one of the first travellers to visit Zermatt and he recorded his impressions of the Matterhorn.

When the Professor offered his reward in 1760 no one made any serious attempt to gain it. None of the local peasantry had any desire to reach the summit of a mountain reputed to be guarded by Alpine dragons, which many people, including educated persons, claimed to have seen.

The first serious attempt was made in July 1775, by four natives of Chamonix: Jean-Nicolas Couteran, whose mother was the innkeeper at Chamonix, was the leader, and there were three guides, Victor Tissai and François and Michel Paccard, cousins of the Dr Paccard who was eventually to be one of the first men to stand on the summit. They almost reached the Dôme du Goûter on the North-West Ridge, at a height of 4,304m,

PETITS ROCHERS ROUGES ROCHERS ROUGES PETITS MULETS JANSSEN'S OBSERVATORY GRAND PLATEAU LA TOURNETTE LOSSES DU DROMADAIRE

CABANE VALLOT

GRANDS MULETS

Mont Blanc, a diagrammatic sketch by Edward Whymper of the route

503m below the summit.

Eight years later, in 1783, three young guides from Chamonix, Joseph Carrier, Jean-Marie Couttet and Jean-Baptiste Lombard, made a determined effort to reach the summit. They got as far as the foot of the Dôme du Goûter where Couttet was overcome by the heat and the expedition turned back. On his return to Chamonix, Lombard announced that if he attempted the climb again he would take a parasol and a bottle of scent to combat the heat!

That same year, Paccard, then an eighteen-year-old medical student of Sallanches, further down the valley from Chamonix, made the first, guideless attempt on the mountain together with Thomas Blaikie, a Scottish botanist, landscape gardener and ardent walker, reaching a point high up under the Aiguille du Goûter, north westwards of the Dôme du Goûter. It was the first of Paccard's five or six attempts on the summit. Later he became the local doctor at Chamonix.

Between autumn of 1784 and August 1786 so many attempts were made on the mountain that it is impossible even to summarise them here.

The amount of equipment carried is always interesting. In the first mass attack by a party, which included Professor de Saussure, five porters and at least nine guides, in August 1787, two mattresses and bedding weighing some 150lb and loads of firewood were taken in addition to provisions and scientific instruments. In June 1786, as a result of a wager, two parties of guides set out, joined, uninvited, by Jacques Balmat, a twenty-four-year-old crystal hunter, and 'a narrow and covetous man' as described by a fellow countryman. They reached the Rochers Vallot on the north-west ridge beyond the Col du Dôme at 4,237m. These rocks are at the foot of the final arête, the Bosses Arête. On this attempt Balmat was benighted alone, probably on the Grand Plateau. The best route to the top was, however, becoming clear and victory was close, although it was not to be won by the so-called primitive route, by way of the Dôme.

On the Mer de Glace in the 1860s. Note the lady's costume on the right (*RTHL*)

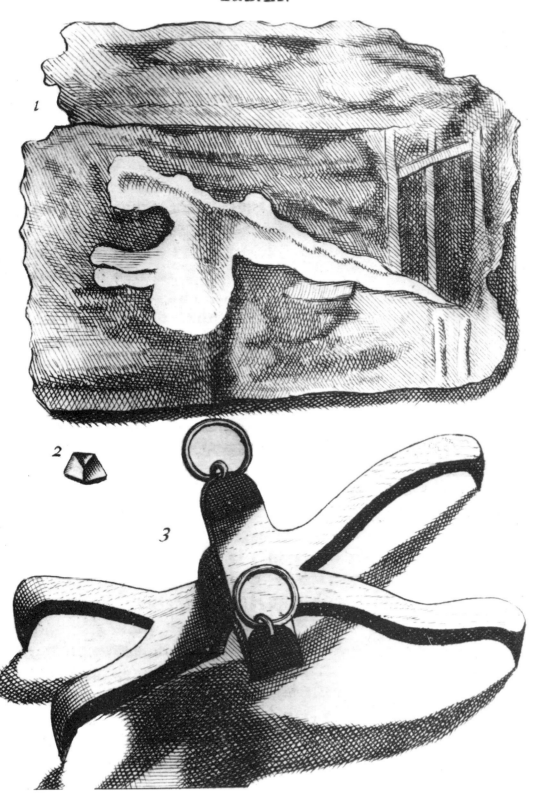

Tab. IX.

Swiss climbing iron of 1723.
Earliest known picture in the
Alpine Club's archives of this
climbing aid (*Alpine Club*)

3 Conquest of Mont Blanc

When Dr Paccard set off from Chamonix at about 3.30 pm on Monday, 7 August 1786 for what was to be the conquest of Mont Blanc, he had already decided two things: that he would bivouac on the top, and by which route he would gain it.

His decision to try a new and unknown route which would take him to a point high on the north-east ridge, instead of using the so-called 'primitive route', by way of the Taconnaz Glacier and the Dôme du Goûter on the North-West Ridge, was probably influenced by the gloomy report given by Pierre Balmat, one of the leaders of an expedition made by two local guides in June

Jacques Balmat. After his first ascent of Mont Blanc in 1786 he climbed it again in 1787 with Professor de Saussure who had offered a reward in 1760 for a serious attempt

1786, to Professor de Saussure, about the apparent impregnability of the Bosses Arête, the final ridge between the Dôme du Goûter and the summit.

For three years Dr Paccard had been keeping the north face of the mountain under observation by telescope from the Brévent, the remarkable and now world-famous view-point on the north side of the valley above Chamonix, and with this he had been able to observe the frequency and direction of the avalanches and ice-falls onto the Grand Plateau which lies below the summit between the North-East and North-West Ridges.

His companion was Jacques Balmat, a local man who had been benighted alone during the guides' expedition of June 1786. He had asked Dr Paccard to take him on the climb and this the doctor had agreed to do, not as a guide but as a porter. Why he took a man as generally unpopular as Balmat, and with such a disagreeable nature, when there was such a large choice open to him is not clear. Balmat himself was so anxious for glory and the prize money offered by Professor de Saussure twenty-six years previously, that he actually set out to climb the mountain while his baby daughter was mortally ill. She died the following day while he was still on the mountain.

Paccard's principal interest in the climb was scientific. He wanted to prove that Mont Blanc was higher than the then generally accepted height of 4,777m.

In the afternoon of 7 August, Dr Paccard marked his barometer with a diamond at the level at which the mercury stood at Chamonix. He had to do this because it was an ungraduated instrument, and he continued to record levels in this way until he reached the summit. In the village the recorded level shown was the equivalent of 1,037m (by the conversion of the height of a column of mercury into altitude above sea level) which was approximately correct.

It was now about 3.30 pm, and he then set off to meet Balmat at Le Mont, a hamlet at the foot of the Montagne de la Côte, the long approach ridge leading up from the valley to the Bossons and Taconnaz Glaciers. With him he had some food, writing materials, a compass, the barometer, a Réaumur thermometer and an iron-shod glacier pole. Balmat was carrying a sack containing bread and meat, and a similar pole. They must also have had at least one blanket between them.

By 9 pm the two men had reached an altitude on the Montagne de la Côte which the Doctor calculated with his barometer to be 2,392m. Here, they bivouacked.

The weather had been changeable, with the wind from the north west and cloud which from time to time obscured the summit; but now the sky was cloudless and there was a bright moon.

The temperature was unnaturally high for such an altitude, 13° Réaumur by Paccard's thermometer, the equivalent of 61.25°F, which augured badly for the crossing of the crevasses on the glaciers and for ascending the snow-slopes.

They set off at 4.30 am the following morning (the 8th). The sky was still cloudless Even at this early hour the temperature was still far too high, 6° Réaumur, the equivalent of 45.5°F. At 5 am they reached the head of the Côte. There, by the boulders which are a feature of the place, the barometer recorded an equivalent to an altitude of 2,611m. (It is, according to modern maps, 2,530m and is known as Le Gîte—resting place—à Balmat.) The wind was now north, the best possible direction for the attempt and it continued to blow from this direction for the rest of the day. They now entered the Jonction, the labyrinth of *séracs* (ice pinnacles) and crevasses at the meeting place of the Bossons and Taconnaz Glaciers, between the head of the

Montagne de la Côte and the rocks known as the Grands Mulets. These rocks, at the foot of the long ridge which divides the two glaciers, now lay some 900m (1,000yd) ahead of them.

As Paccard had feared, due to the abnormally high temperature the snow bridges over the crevasses were in an extremely dangerous condition and on four separate occasions he and Balmat only saved themselves from plunging into the depths below by the expedient of falling flat on their faces when they felt the snow giving way beneath their feet, at the same time spanning the gulf with their glacier poles. This hair-raising technique could of course only be employed on narrow crevasses—the larger ones had to be circumvented.

In this way it took them five hours to force the Jonction and when they had succeeded in doing so they found themselves far out to the west of the Grands Mulets on the Taconnaz Glacier. The snow on the glacier was relatively smooth; but it was also very

Dr Michel-Gabriel Paccard who, with Jacques Balmat, made the first ascent of Mont Blanc. (Note the mis-spellings of names in both engravings) (*Alpine Club*)

J. M. Cachat, nicknamed 'Le Géant', was a leading guide at Chamonix in the late eighteenth century (*Alpine Club*)

soft, and it became increasingly difficult to climb as the sun warmed it.

They went up the glacier past what are now known as the Rocher Pitschner and the Rocher de l'Heureux Retour, outcrops on the ridge which separates the Taconnaz from the Bossons Glacier to the east, until they reached what are now known as the Petites Montées, steep snow-slopes leading up to the Petit Plateau, which lies below the Grand Plateau.

Here, at a height of about 3,350m, they halted to eat a meal. It was about midday and while eating they saw a live butterfly on the snow, and another small insect.

Dr Paccard again marked the tube of the barometer which now registered the equivalent of a height of 3,508m, an error of more than 150m. This was probably due to the battering it had received during the passage through the Jonction, which had caused it to spring a leak, admitting air. It continued to give readings that were too high as far as the summit; but fortunately for the Doctor's peace of mind he did not know this at the time.

By now Balmat had probably begun to realise that Dr Paccard had no intention of following the primitive route to the Dôme, or of following any other route to the North-West Ridge.

At 12.30 pm they began the ascent of the Petites Montées towards the Petit Plateau and on reaching it were confronted by an ice-fall from the Dôme du Goûter which forced them to make a detour. From the Petit Plateau they began the steeper ascent of the Grandes Montées to the Grand Plateau.

At 1.52 pm, as Paccard noted, they had reached a point just below a large crevasse which guarded the foot of the Grand Plateau, and here he again checked the temperature which had fallen to $11\frac{1}{2}°$ Réaumur (equal to 64.5°F).

Here, the head of the Bossons Glacier was on their left, and they were at a height of between 3,825 and 3,850m, although Paccard's barometer registered the equivalent to 3,997m.

They turned the end of the crevasse and emerged onto the Grand Plateau, about a kilometre long, between the point where they arrived on it and the foot of the North-East Ridge on the far side.

The crossing of the Plateau, with the wind now strong on their backs, was rendered difficult by the state of the snow which had frozen on the surface although not sufficiently to prevent them from crashing through into the soft snow underneath. Here, Balmat led the way, with Paccard directing him, towards the foot of the North-East Ridge.

The realisation that Paccard intended to climb it led Balmat, who had certainly never lacked courage, to tell Paccard at 3 pm that he would go no further. Nevertheless, as he wrote later in his signed affidavit, 'he [the Doctor] never ceased from encouraging me', and this was one of the moments when Paccard required all his powers of persuasion, in fact it was the crucial moment of the climb.

The Bossons glacier below the Dôme and Aiguille du Goûter (*John Topham*)

Balmat allowed himself to be persuaded; Paccard took part of Balmat's load, although at which point it is not clear, and now Paccard took the lead up what was to be, apart from the Jonction, the most difficult part of the entire climb, the ascent of what was subsequently named the Lower Ancien Passage (Ancien Passage Inférieur).

The Passage, hardly ever used since Dr Paccard's climb in 1786, is the most steep and difficult of the four principal routes from the Grand Plateau to the summit. It leads up at an angle of about 32 degrees, by way of a series of small ice-cliffs between two long ribs of red rock, the Rochers Rouges, which originate on the North-East Ridge and descend from it to the Grand Plateau.

They reached the foot of the Passage at 3.30 pm and there they halted while Paccard again noted the temperature (6° Réaumur, 45.5°F) and the barometric pressure, which was equivalent to an altitude of 4,295m, again more than the true altitude which was between 4,080 and 4,100m (13,386–13,452ft).

He now led the way up the 345m Passage which was now in shadow, an exposed climb for men without a rope. It took them one and a half hours and at the end of that time they emerged from it at a height of 4,447m, 360m below the summit, from which they were separated by steep but not difficult snow-slopes.

It was now 5 pm and for the first time they came under observation from below, where, among other watchers, the Baron Adolf Traugott von Gersdorf, a chance German visitor and the possessor of an excellent telescope, saw them moving rapidly towards the summit before being lost to view. At this late hour Paccard ordered Balmat to search for a suitable place to bivouac below the ridge while he went on to examine some rocks. Balmat failed to discover a sufficiently sheltered spot and Paccard decided to go for the summit.

Taking turns to lead, they again came into view below the Petits Rochers Rouges, a group of rocks at a height of 4,577m, where they halted. The wind was now so strong that, in spite of being secured by a cord, Dr Paccard's hat was blown away. They halted again at the Petits Mulets, another small group of rocks, at 4,690m where the Doctor collected some rock specimens distinguished by having vertical laminiae (the thinnest separable layers in stratified rock deposits).

At 6.12 pm the two men began the final climb to the summit. It was 117m (384 vertical ft) and those below saw them literally running for the summit: Paccard on a direct line towards it; Balmat, by a zig-zag route, which held him back. At 6.32 pm Paccard reached the summit, immediately followed by Balmat. In Balmat's words, which formed part of his affidavit, 'My detour delayed me, and I had to run in order to reach the summit nearly at the same time'. They had covered the last 117m in eleven minutes, after an ascent of 2,474m, which had taken more than fourteen hours.

There is no record of what they said to one another. Paccard planted a stick in the snow to which he attached a red handkerchief seen by the watchers below. The only other living things were two choughs on the wing.

Then he set about making the observations on which he had set his heart. The barometer indicated a height for the summit of 5,039m, 232m too high, and the temperature was '6 degres sous 0' (18.5°F), sufficient to cause frostbite, particularly with a freezing north wind blowing.

It was now about 6.45 pm and in the hope of discovering a place for a bivouac, for the sun was now setting, they descended the short, south-east ridge which leads towards the lesser summit of Mont Blanc de Courmayeur. They failed to find a suitable place and at a point midway between the two peaks they turned back.

Just before 7 pm they were again seen by Baron von Gersdorf, 9km away, running or glissading down to the Petits Rochers Rouges, which they reached in six minutes. From then on they were lost to view.

The descent itself was a remarkable feat by men who by now must have been exhausted, and were also frostbitten: first by the Ancien Passage, a hazardous affair for unroped men in the twilight; then by way of the Grand and Petit Plateaux to the Taconnaz Glacier with night already upon them. Fortunately, the moon rose early, it was almost full, otherwise the crossing of the crevasses in the Jonction would have been a hazardous business indeed. As it was, Paccard finally broke his barometer there. By midnight they were at the head of the Montagne de la Côte, where they bivouacked by the rocks.

By this time one of Paccard's hands was black from frostbite and one of Balmat's white. This was not coincidence but simply because in the course of forcing the Ancien Passage Paccard's leather gloves had become so soaked through contact with the ice that he had lost all feeling in his hands and had borrowed one of Balmat's furlined gloves in order to be able to continue leading the climb. Now they massaged each other's hands with snow until they became a normal colour.

The next morning Paccard was almost completely snow-blind and Balmat had to lead him down the mountain to the valley. Once there, each man went his own way, Balmat to his house at Les Baux to find his child dead, Paccard to his father's house at Chamonix which he reached at 8 am with great difficulty. There he went to bed.

So ended this courageous and remarkable exploit, during which Paccard and Balmat had climbed a height of 2,438m and descended the same vertical distance in the course of nineteen and three-quarter hours.

As T. Graham Brown and Sir Gavin de Beer, the authors of that fascinating work of detection, *The First Ascent of Mont Blanc*, wrote:

The complete ascent of Mont Blanc direct from Chamonix, one of 12,369ft, has occasionally been achieved in more recent times, and even with return to Chamonix

on the same day. But the men who have achieved this striking athletic feat were lightly laden, they used the established route by which most of the difficulties of the Jonction are avoided, and they had the benefit of ladders over the crevasses and a well-trodden track elsewhere. In comparison Dr Paccard and Balmat were handicapped, as it were, by the effort-wasting difficulties of the Jonction, by heavy and awkward loads, and by soft new snow on an untrodden track. If allowance is made for these disadvantages, the first ascent of Mont Blanc must be reckoned amongst the greatest feats, and exhibitions of determination, in Alpine history; and to the mere bodily stamina which was required of the two men, there must be added (especially in the case of Dr Paccard) the mental effort which was needed for the conquest

of doubts and anxieties, and for taking and maintaining the brave decisions to go forward in spite of the lateness of the hour and of the unknown risks to life which there might be at high altitude.

It would be pleasant to leave the protagonists at this point, each to enjoy his glory according to his own bent; but unfortunately Dr Paccard was not to have this pleasure, although Balmat did receive his reward from Professor de Saussure.

In September 1786, Bourrit, rendered almost insanely jealous by the news of Dr Paccard's victory, published a scurrilous pamphlet in which he wrote that it had been Balmat who had discovered the Lower Ancien Passage during the double attack by the guides in June 1786. This was the expedition on which Balmat got left behind and

On the summit of Mont Blanc. Cloud clings to the Grandes Jorasses. In the far distance on the right are Weisshorn, the Mischabel Peaks, the Grand Combin and the Matterhorn on the extreme right (*John Cleare*)

passed the night alone, most probably on the Grand Plateau.

In his pamphlet Bourrit declared that Balmat had thus discovered the route after passing a night 'at a height greater than that of the Dôme du Goûter . . . Having descended to Chamonix,' the pamphlet continued, 'to the relief of his companions who had thought that he must have fallen, he was visited by Dr Paccard, to whom he confided his observations and experiences.'

As a result of this, according to Bourrit, Balmat offered to take Paccard to the top.

There followed a description of the climb which culminated in Dr Paccard sinking down exhausted in the snow while Balmat went on to the summit, returning to drag the semi-comatose Paccard up to it, also.

None of this nonsense, of Bourrit's creation, could have been written without Balmat's tacit approval yet in spite of this, on 18 October that same year (1786), Balmat signed an affidavit in which he affirmed that Dr Paccard had been the leader, that the route had been of his discovering, and that he had been encouraged by Paccard to go on and that Paccard had been the first, by a short head, to reach the summit, and in May 1787, Paccard arranged for the publication of this affidavit in the *Journal de Lausanne*. In July that year Balmat suggested, in a public confrontation in a street in Chamonix, that Dr Paccard had forced him to sign a blank affidavit. Dr Paccard knocked him down with his umbrella.

In 1787, Colonel Mark Beaufoy, an Englishman, was the first foreigner to reach the summit of Mont Blanc; a Chamonix maidservant Marie Paradis, the first woman in 1808, and William Howard and Jeremiah van Rensselaer the first Americans on what was the tenth ascent, on 12 July 1819.

4 Before the Golden Age

The so-called 'Golden Age' of mountaineering, when climbing became a sport, is generally accepted to have begun in 1856, the year before the formation of the British Alpine Club and the year of the publication of Alfred Wills' *Wanderings Among the High Alps*, in which he described in a most readable way his ascent of the Wetterhorn in 1854. However it would be utterly wrong to think that the climbing of mountains ceased in the years after Paccard and Balmat's ascent of Mont Blanc in 1786 or that Mont Blanc was the only peak which engaged the attention of climbers.

William Augustus Brevoort Coolidge, a great historian of the mountains, as well as being a notable climber, listed 132 Alpine peaks climbed before Wills' climb of the Wetterhorn, including the Wetterhorn itself.

One of the Dents du Midi, 3,257m (10,696ft) in Switzerland was climbed in the same year as the Aiguille and the Dôme du Goûter (1784) by Clément, Curé of the Val d'Illicz.

Chamois hunter, 1825. Many of the early guides had come to know the Alps as hunters and were in fact the early mountaineers. This one wears climbing irons very similar to the one illustrated on page 19 (*Alpine Club*)

The Ortler, the highest peak in the Tirol (3,899m), now in Italian territory, was climbed by a chamois-hunter, Joseph Pichler, in 1804 and an Austrian party ascended the Gross Venediger 3,797m (12,008ft) in 1841. Meanwhile, between 1788 and 1824, the great Swiss climber, the Benedictine monk, Father Placidus à Spescha, of the monastery of Disentis in the Grisons, had nine climbing seasons in the course of which he made first ascents of the Stockgron (3,418m) in 1788; the Rheinwaldhorn (3,398m) in 1789; the Oberalpstock (3,332m) in 1792, Piz Urlaun (3,538.6m) in 1793 and others including the Güferhorn (3,393m) in 1806. At his instigation the Tödi, 3,620m, the highest peak in the Glarner Alps was climbed for the first time. In 1822 two Scottish ladies, Mrs and Miss Campbell, succeeded in crossing the Col du Géant, between Chamonix and Courmayeur, a remarkable feat. In 1811 Johann Rudolph and Hieronymus Meyer, sons of a rich merchant of Aarau, who had himself climbed the Titlis, 3,239m, reached the summit of the Jungfrau, (4,158m). The Finsteraarhorn, the highest peak in the Oberland in the Eastern Bernese Alps, (4,274m), was finally completely conquered in 1829 by two guides, Jakob Leuthold and Johann Währen, who were accompanied by a Swiss scientist, F. J. Hugi, up to about 60m below the summit.

In 1801 the Punta Giordani (4,046m), one of the ten peaks of Monte Rosa, was climbed by Dr Pietro Giordani of Alagna. Another of its peaks, the Pyramide Vincent (4,215m), was climbed in 1819 and the Punta Gnifetti (Signalkuppe) 4,556m was climbed by Giovanni Gnifetti, the priest of Alagna, in 1842.

In 1821 a company of registered guides (the CGG) was formed at Chamonix. A not very difficult test of competency was instituted, basic charges, extremely high, were laid down, as were the numbers of guides who

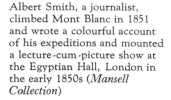

Albert Smith, a journalist, climbed Mont Blanc in 1851 and wrote a colourful account of his expeditions and mounted a lecture-cum-picture show at the Egyptian Hall, London in the early 1850s (*Mansell Collection*)

were to accompany each amateur (four to the summit for each climber).

In 1820 J. Zumstein, a great Valaisian climber, had made five attempts on the summit of Monte Rosa, the Dufourspitze (4,634m), In the course of one of them, he slept out in a crevasse near the top, before reaching the summit of one of the group, subsequently named the Zumsteinspitze, (4,563m, 15,004ft).

In 1848, the French climber Victor Puiseux, reached the top of Mont Pelvoux, 3,946m (12,073ft) in the Dauphiné and two years later a Swiss climber, named Coaz, climbed the Piz Bernina (4,049m, 13,285ft), the highest peak in the Engadine.

What gave great impetus to the growth of interest in mountains in the English-speaking world were the writings of the author and artist, John Ruskin (1819–1900).

Ruskin's enthusiasm for mountain scenery began in 1824, when he visited the Lake District and Scotland, travelling with his parents in a private carriage, at which time he was only five years old.

In 1833, when still only fourteen, he had his first sight of the Alps. 'For me,' he wrote, 'the Alps and their people were alike beautiful in their snow and their humanity; and I wanted neither for them nor myself sight of any thrones in heaven but the rocks, or any of spirits in heaven but the clouds.'

These sentiments, so far removed from the conception that had ruled up to then of mountain scenery as being 'horrid' or 'awful' in the Gothic sense of the words, he communicated to the public in the famous fourth volume of his *Modern Painters*. Nevertheless, with some notable exceptions, he failed to ingratiate himself with the Victorian climbers as a whole, partly because he himself was no climber—he believed that 'the Alps were on the whole, best seen from below', and also because he deplored what he

Mr Albert Smith's 'Ascent of Mont Blanc' as projected on the screen at the Egyptian Hall. The crevasse being perilously crossed is in the Taconnaz Glacier (*Mansell Collection*)

Drawing of a glacier table by James David Forbes, a scientist, who carried out experiments in glacier movement. His friendly relationship with Jacques Balmat's great-nephew was to be a pattern of such relationships between Victorian climbers and their guides (*Alpine Club*)

regarded as the philistine attitude of the new breed of climbers,

> the extreme vanity of the modern Englishman in making a momentary Stylites of himself on the top of a Horn or an Aiguille, and his occasional confession of a charm in the solitude of the rocks, of which he modifies nevertheless the poignancy with his pocket newspaper, and from the prolongation of which he thankfully escapes to the nearest table-d'hôte.

Another writer, of a very different sort to Ruskin, but who nevertheless drew popular attention to mountaineering, was Albert Smith, a journalist who after several attempts succeeded in climbing Mont Blanc in 1851, an expedition of which he wrote a colourful account in *The Story of Mont Blanc*, published in 1853. Smith mounted a sort of lecture-cum-picture show, with the pictures projected on an enormous screen, at the Egyptian Hall in London, complete with girls in Swiss mountain costume and St Bernard dogs, one of which scared the daylights out of Queen Victoria. This entertainment ran for six years.

A third important man in the history of modern mountaineering was James David Forbes (1809–68) the youngest son of a Scottish baronet. He was a scientist and visited Chamonix for the first time in 1846 where he carried out experiments in the movements of glaciers with the help of the great guide Auguste Balmat, great nephew of that Jacques Balmat who had climbed Mont Blanc. The friendly relationship which he formed with Balmat was to be a pattern for many similar friendships forged between the Victorian climbers and their guides. Not only was Forbes a distinguished scientist—his theory of the movement of glaciers proved to be the correct one—but he was able to communicate to a wide public the wonder of the mountains through his *Travels through the Alps of Savoy and other parts of the Pennine Chain, with Observations on the Phenomena of the Glaciers* (1843).

A picture from James Forbes's *Travels through the Alps of Savoy* demonstrating his measuring of the angle between a section of the Mer de Glace and the rock, near Montanvert (*Alpine Club*)

5 The Golden Age

The eleven years following Wills' successful attempt on the Wetterhorn in 1854, span what has come to be known as the Golden Age of mountaineering. In the course of them, climbing became widely recognised as a sport, although a hazardous one, and was pursued with such enthusiasm that by the end of the season of 1865 almost every major Alpine peak had been scaled at least once. During this period most of the climbers were British and for the most part were accompanied by guides. The Alpine Club was founded in 1857 in London and it is some

'F. Boileau and Hon W. Vernon on return from a mountain expedition.' So reads the caption in pencil of this photograph taken at Vevey in 1858. Although their costume and equipment suggest an afternoon on the river rather than a climb, they may well have changed before the picture was taken (*Mansell Collection*)

measure of the greater interest taken by the British in climbing at this time, in comparison with other Europeans, that five years were to elapse before the Austrians founded an Alpine Club, six before the Swiss founded theirs (1863), while the German and the French clubs were not founded until 1869 and 1874.

Between 1858 and 1865 more than eighty first ascents and crossings of passes were made by climbers who were either already members of the British club or who subsequently became members. Men such as Francis

Fox Tuckett, a Bristol businessman, were not only making first ascents, but opening up remote regions such as the Dauphiné Alps, a westerly extension of the Cottian Alps in France, subsequently further exploited by Moore and Whymper on a joint expedition in 1864. Tuckett had taken up mountaineering for scientific as well as recreational reasons. He 'was a sight to see,' the Reverend F. J. A. Hort, a scholar and Professor of Divinity at Cambridge, who took an active part in the foundation of the Alpine Club, wrote in 1861,

being hung from head to foot with 'notions' in the strictest sense of the word, several of them being inventions of his own. Besides such commonplace things as a great axe-head and a huge rope and thermometers, he had two barometers, a sypsieometer, and a wonderful apparatus, pot within pot, for boiling water at great heights, first for scientific and then for culinary purposes.

Tuckett also climbed extensively in other then unknown regions of Corsica, Greece, Norway, the Pyrenees and Algeria and the Alpine Club Register credits him with 269 peaks and 687 passes to his death in 1913.

During these eleven years a number of peaks which had already been climbed previously were also ascended by other, often more difficult routes. Two examples are the (then) hazardous ascent of the Jungfrau from the Rothtal above Lauterbrunnen in 1864, and the following year a successful attempt to reach the summit of Mont Blanc by way of the

The Brenva Face on the Italian side of Mont Blanc, scene of many of the classic Alpine ice climbs. *Left*, Mont Blanc de Courmayeur; *right*, Mont Blanc (*John Cleare*)

Brenva Face on the eastern, Italian, side of the massif.

Although it is impossible and invidious to attempt to list or even summarise the activities of all the outstanding climbers of the period it is perhaps worthwhile giving the composition of the parties engaged in the attack on these two peaks as each member of it was a great climber and together they form a typical cross-section of the kind of men who were climbing at the time.

Among the party on the Jungfrau were (Sir) Leslie Stephen, the distinguished literary critic, editor of the *Dictionary of National Biography* and the father of the novelist Virginia Woolfe. Until he married, in 1867, he had an amazing record of first ascents, traverses and crossings from 1858 onwards, which included the first complete ascent of Mont Blanc by way of the Dôme du Goûter; Florence Craufurd Grove (a man) who, in 1867, became the first amateur to ascend the Matterhorn by way of the Italian Ridge. It was of this ridge which the great guide Jean-

33

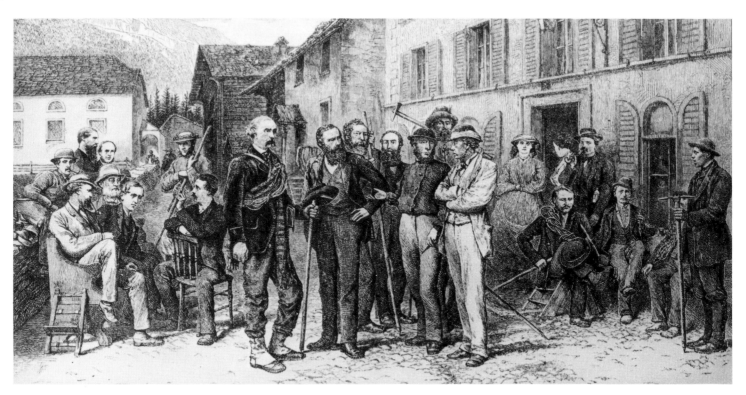

Outside the Monte Rosa Hotel, Zermatt, where the Alpinists had a club room, stand some eminent climbers: Sir Leslie Stephen (sitting left, hand on knee), President of the Alpine Club in 1866; John Ball (centre left with gaiters), first President of the Alpine Club; Ulrich Lauener, the famous guide (backright with ice axe); Alfred Wills who climbed the Wetterhorn (centre right in white); and the only woman in the group, probably Lucy Walker, stands by the door. She was one of the first notable women Alpinists (*Alpine Club and Swiss Tourist Office*)

Antoine Carrel, who reached the summit by it with J. Baptiste Bich in July 1865, told Whymper, when asked if he had ever done anything more difficult, 'Man cannot do anything much more difficult than that'. Whymper himself recorded his opinion that it was 'the most desperate piece of mountain-scrambling upon record'. The other two members of the party were Reginald Mac-donald, the first man to climb the Aiguille de Bionnassay (4,052m) in the Mont Blanc range; and the famous guides, Melchior and Jakob Anderegg. On the Brenva Face of Mont Blanc the party consisted of Adolphus Warburton Moore, a senior official at the India Office and one of the greatest of Victorian climbers who, between June 1864 and July 1865 alone, made nine first ascents and crossings, five of them with Edward Whymper; Francis Walker, a Liverpool merchant, who did not take up climbing until he was fifty, and was then fifty-seven; his son Horace Walker, whose first ascents and crossings cover six pages of the *Alpine Club Register;* George Spencer Mathews, a Birmingham estate and land agent, one of three brothers, all climbers—another, William, was one of those responsible for the foundation of the Alpine Club, the third, Charles Edward, besides being an enthusiastic Alpinist, did much to improve the status of the Alpine guides, as well as being one of the founders of Welsh climbing (he climbed both Snowdon and Cader Idris more than 100 times). The two guides on this attack on the Brenva Face were Melchior and Jakob Anderegg who were cousins and it was of Melchior that Charles Mathews wrote:

He first taught me how to climb. For more than 20 seasons he has led me—in success and failure—in sunshine and in storm. He has rejoiced with me in happy times; he has nursed me when suffering from accident with a charming devotion. Year after year I have met him with keener pleasure. Year after year I have parted with him with deeper regret.

(Quoted in *The Victorian Mountaineers*, Ronald Clark, 1953)

The first British women climbers whose names have come down to us were the three Misses Parminter who climbed on Le Buet (3,099m) in the Savoie Alps in about 1799, the mountain which, the following year, became the scene of the first known death of a climber in a crevasse, a Dane, F. A. Eschen. In 1822, Mrs and Miss Campbell made their remarkable crossing of the Col du Géant from Chamonix to Courmayeur. They had the intention of attempting Mont Blanc but, unfortunately, never returned to Chamonix.

Two women climbers whose careers began in the Golden Age were the American, Miss Meta Brevoort, and Miss Lucy Walker. Miss Brevoort was the aunt of William Augustus Brevoort Coolidge with whom she subsequently made many climbs until her death in 1876, often in company with their dog, Tschingel. Miss Brevoort sometimes wore trousers in desperation—dress was one of the great impediments to Victorian lady climbers. It is recorded of Ulrich Lauener, the great guide, that he crossed the Strahlegg Pass with his employer's crinoline over one shoulder the rope negligently over the other. 'Small rings should be sewn inside the seam of the dress', one notable woman mountain traveller of the 1850s, Mrs Cole, advised, 'and a cord passed through them, the ends of which should be knotted together in such a way that the whole dress may be drawn up at moment's notice the required height. A riding skirt, without a body, which can be slipped off and on in a moment, is also invaluable.' Nevertheless, Miss Brevoort complained that, even so, 'snow enters the rings and stuffs up the hem and makes me heavy and wet. I have had to baste up both dress and skirt.'

Lucy Walker was the daughter of Francis Walker of the Liverpool climbing family. In 1864 she made the first ascent of the Balmhorn (by the south-west arête) together with her father, her brother Horace and the two Andereggs. This was the first major first

Three famous guides of the 1860s: Peter Perren of Zermatt, Christian Almer of Grindelwald and Melchior Anderegg of Meiringen (*Swiss Tourist Office*)

Lucy Walker, first woman to climb the Matterhorn, with her brother, Horace. While climbing Lucy ate only spongecake and drank only champagne. Her glass is being filled by the unknown gentleman behind (*RTHL*)

The Eiger and Mönch. A watercolour by Edward Whymper, who, apart from being the eminent climber of his day, was a wood engraver by profession and an artist (*Alpine Club*)

ascent made by a woman (Mrs Emma Winkworth, the wife of Stephen Winkworth, a spinner of Bolton, had made the first ascents by a woman of the Aletschhorn, the second highest of the Oberland peaks, and the Jungfrau with her husband the previous year, 1863). In 1864 Miss Walker made the fourth ascent of the Eiger (by the West Ridge and Face), and the following year she made the second crossing of the difficult Moming Pass (3,793m, 12,444ft), between the Zinal Rothhorn and the Schallihorn in the Valais (first crossed by Edward Whymper in 1864), in company with Adolphus Moore, Michel Croz, a great Chamonix guide and Christian Almer. She later, in 1871, became the first woman to climb the Matterhorn, thus thwarting an ambition held by Miss Brevoort. Miss Walker invariably wore women's clothes for climbing and while doing so lived on an exclusive diet of sponge cake and champagne or, if none was available, Asti Spumante. Her other sport was croquet. In the course of her climbing career, which covered twenty-one years, she made ninety-eight expeditions, all but three of them successful.

Another great woman climber of the period was Miss Emmeline Lewis Lloyd, a fat, jolly girl who was also a great salmon-fisher in her native Wales. Her climbing companion for a time was Miss Isabella Straton who had an income of £4,000 a year. She began climbing in 1861, aged twenty-three, in the Mont Blanc Range, and ten years later made the first ascent of the Aiguille du Moine between the Mer de Glace and the Glacier de Talèfre; of the Punta Isabella, then named after her, in 1875, and the Aiguille de la Persévérance, the same year. In 1876 she made the first winter ascent of Mont Blanc with Jean Charlet, a Chamonix guide with whom she climbed from 1865 onwards and married. With him she made four ascents of the mountain and also climbed in the Pyrenees. They lived at Argentière, near Chamonix, and she bore him two sons, both of whom climbed Mont Blanc while still children—one aged thirteen, the other eleven and a half.

One of the phenomena of the Victorian Age was the number of clergymen who climbed—the embodiment of muscular Christianity. When Edward Shirley Kennedy (a well known, guideless climber who, in 1855, made the first guideless ascent of Mont Blanc

The certificate issued to successful ascenders of Mont Blanc. The name filled in is Thomas Henry Philpott who made many successful ascents 1861–6 (*Alpine Club*)

Aug 20. 1866.

Eiger and Mönch from the Wengern Alp

The Matterhorn to the Eiger, from a panorama in Baedeker's *Switzerland* of 1893. The crosses mark (*left to right*): Matterhorn, Weisshorn, Mont Blanc, Nesthorn, Aletschhorn, Jungfrau, Eiger

PANORAMA VON EGGISHORN.

and the first from St Gervais, together with the Reverend Charles Hudson, himself one of the great pioneers) circularised climbers before the formation of the Alpine Club in 1857, more than a quarter of those who replied that they would like to become members were clergymen. Among them were the Reverend James Hornby and the Reverend Thomas Philpott who, among their other first ascents and crossings between 1861 and 1866, traversed the Aletschhorn (4,195m), and made the second ascent of the Lauterbrunnen Breithorn, reaching the summit a bare ten minutes after the great Swiss climber and mineralogist, Edmund von Fellenberg of Bern, the first secretary of the Swiss Alpine Club.

Another famous pair of clergymen climbers were the brothers James Grenville and Christopher Smyth who began the first exploration among the Zermatt peaks in 1854–55, making the first ascent of the Strahlhorn (4,190m), the first British ascent of the Ostspitze of Monte Rosa, both with Edmund Smyth, and in 1855 of the highest summit, the Dufourspitze (4,634m), in company with E. J. W. Stevenson, the Reverend Hudson, Ulrich Lauener and Johann and Matthias Zumtaugwald. Even Leslie Stephen took Holy Orders, although he was forced to do so, having been made a Wrangler of Trinity Hall in 1854. He abandoned the Church and resigned his Fellowship as a result in 1862. Some words of Edward Whymper from his bestseller, *Scrambles Amongst the Alps* sum up what the climbers of the Victorian Age felt about their pastime.

We glory in the physical regeneration which is the product of our exertions; we exult over the grandeur of the scenes that are brought before our eyes, the splendours of sunrise and sunset, and the beauties of hill, dale, lake, wood and waterfall; but we value more highly the development of manliness, and the evolution, under combat with difficulties, of those noble qualities of human nature—courage, patience, endurance, and fortitude.

The 1860s saw the beginning of guideless climbing by the three Parker brothers of Liverpool—Charles Stuart, a British MP, Samuel Sandbach and Alfred Traill Parker, both of whom were in the family shipping business. They had begun climbing on Skye in the 1850s. In July 1860 they reached 3,505m and in 1861, 3,566m on the East Face of the Matterhorn (the Zermatt side) before being forced back principally by bad weather. In 1865, the year the Matterhorn was finally conquered, they made the first guideless ascent of the Finsteraarhorn.

The Reverend Arthur Gilbert Girdlestone made the first guideless ascent of the Wetterhorn in 1867, but his book, *The High Alps Without Guides*, did nothing but reinforce the prejudice against guideless climbing.

Like Tuckett, not all climbers of the Golden Age were dedicated to the purely sporting aspects of climbing. The prickly son of an Irish shoemaker, the scientist, Professor John Tyndall, a contemporary of Faraday who worked with him before succeeding him at the Royal Institution, and

Previous page: The Eiger North Face. Dougal Haston (*upper figure*) and Chris Bonington doing their reconnaissance for the 'Eiger Direct' in the winter of 1968 (*John Cleare*)

The Matterhorn: the Hörnli Ridge (*Leo Dickinson*)

married the niece of the Duke of Abercorn, was, like James David Forbes, originally more concerned with the theory of glaciers and was bitterly opposed by him. His theories were expounded in his *Glaciers of the Alps* (1860). From that time onwards he became increasingly fascinated by climbing for its own sake.

In 1860 he made the first of his two attempts on the Matterhorn, the second being in 1862, on both occasions accompanied among others, by the strange, silent Valaisian guide, Johann-Joseph Bennen of Laax in the upper Rhône Valley, with whom he had climbed the Finsteraarhorn in 1858. In 1861, together with Bennen and an Oberland guide named Wenger, the Professor succeeded in scaling the Weisshorn (14,781ft). They climbed it, after a bivouac, by way of the East Ridge, the difficulties and dangers of which are described by Tyndall in an epic

passage in one of his books *Hours of Exercise in the Alps*, first published in 1871:

The mountain was scarred by long couloirs, filled with clear hard ice. The cutting of steps across these couloirs proved to be so tedious and fatiguing that I urged Bennen to abandon them and try the ridge once more. We regained it and worked along it as before. Here and there upon the northern side the snow was folded over, and we worked slowly upward along the cornice snow. The ridge became gradually narrower, and the precipices on each side more sheer. We reached the end of one of its subdivisions, and found ourselves separated from the next rocks by a gap about twenty yards across. The ridge has here narrowed to a mere wall, which, however, as rock, would present no serious

The Reverend Charles Hudson and his party with their equipment during their ascent of Mont Blanc in 1855. When the Alpine Club was being formed, more than a quarter of those who applied for membership were English clergymen (*Alpine Club*)

difficulty. But upon the wall of rock was placed a second wall of ice, which dwindled to a pure knife-edge at the top. It was white, of very fine grain, and a little moist. How to pass this snow catenary I knew not, for I did not think a human foot could trust itself upon so frail a support. Bennen's practical sagacity, however, came into play. He tried the snow by squeezing it with his foot, and to my astonishment began to cross it. Even after the pressure of his feet the space he had to stand on did not exceed a hand-breadth. I followed him, exactly as a boy walking along a horizontal pole, with toes turned outwards. Right and left the precipices were appalling. We reached the opposite rock, and an earnest smile rippled over Bennen's countenance as he turned towards me. He knew that he had done a daring thing, though not a pre-

sumptous one. 'Had the snow' he said, 'been less perfect, I should not have thought of attempting it; but I knew that after I had set my foot upon the ridge that we might pass without fear. It is quite surprising', the Professor concluded, 'what a number of things the simple observation made by Faraday in 1846 enables us to explain. Bennen's instinctive act is justified by theory. The snow was fine in grain, pure, and moist. When pressed, the attachments of its granules were innumerable, and their perfect cleanness enabled them to freeze together with a maximum energy. It was this freezing which gave the mass its sustaining power. . . . My guide, however, unaided by any theory, did a thing from which I should have shrunk, though backed by all the theories in the world.'

First ascent of the Aiguille du Midi by Ferdinand de Bouillé's guides in the 1860s (*Alpine Club*)

6 Alfred Wills and the Wetterhorn

Both by birth and upbringing Alfred Wills was a typical Victorian climber. He was the son of well-to-do parents, his father was a Justice of the Peace. He became a barrister of the Middle Temple and eventually a judge in the Queen's Bench Division. He owed his appointment as judge to Queen Victoria who insisted to the Prime Minister that the new occupant of the post (the previous one had died of heart failure in a brothel), should be a man of the utmost probity. (It was particularly unfortunate for Oscar Wilde that Wills was the judge who presided over his trial at the Old Bailey.) In the course of his career he was knighted.

At an early age he had become an enthusiastic Alpine traveller, although by the time he married, in 1854, aged twenty-six, he had no really important climbs to his credit. He also had an abiding interest in glaciers, a highly controversial subject at that time, and was a supporter of the theories advanced by Forbes. The honeymoon was spent in Switzerland, the third member of the party being Wills' brother-in-law, and one of their expeditions was to a point high up on the Mer de Glace above Chamonix where they bivouacked. With them went Auguste Balmat, one of the Chamonix guides who specialised at that time in working for visitors with scientific interests.

It was while the party was staying in the Bernese Oberland in the autumn of 1854, that Wills became prey to a temptation all mountaineers are more or less prone to.

'We were staying at Interlaken,' he wrote in *Wanderings Amongst the High Alps*, 'and as I gazed upon the graceful form of the Jungfrau, which rose opposite the window at which I sat, an irrepressible longing came over me to win that lofty and difficult summit, and look down upon the boundless prospect that must stretch on every side. I had crossed many a lofty Col, and wound my way among many a labyrinth of profound and yawning crevasses. I had slept on the moraine of a glacier, and on the peaks which rise in tempting grandeur above the crests of Cols and the summits of the loftiest passes.'

Balmat was enthusiastic and he suggested that they should recruit another guide from Chamonix, a friend of his named Auguste Simond. He was a rough-looking customer of thirty-eight who habitually wore a bowler hat and was so incredibly strong, that he was able to hold a man out at arm's length with one hand. They re-named him Samson.

A third recruit was an Oberlander, Ulrich Lauener, one of four brothers, all famous guides, from the Lauterbrunnen Valley. With one of them, Christian Lauener, Wills had already crossed the Tschingel Pass in 1852. Ulrich was then thirty-three, a huge bearded fellow, vividly described by Wills when he turned up for the first time at the Hotel de la Jungfrau:

We saw a tall, straight, active, knowing-looking fellow, with a cock's feather stuck jauntily in his high-crowned hat, whom I recognised at once as possessing the true Lauener cut, perched on the railings in front of the hotel, lazily dangling his long legs in the air.

Lauener said that it was too late in the season to attempt to climb the Jungfrau, except from the far side of the chain by way of

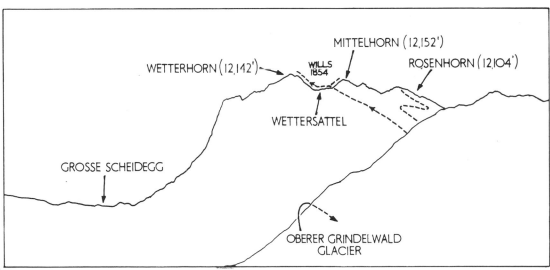

WETTERHORN (12,142')

WILLS 1854

MITTELHORN (12,152')

ROSENHORN (12,104')

WETTERSATTEL

GROSSE SCHEIDEGG

OBERER GRINDELWALD GLACIER

The Wetterhorn seen over the Grindelwald Valley. The key shows the route taken by Wills on his successful ascent, 1854

the Grimsel and the chalets of Merglen, which would take six days, more than Wills could afford on his honeymoon. The Finsteraarhorn and the Schreckhorn were also proposed, but turned down by Lauener on the grounds that it was now too cold to sleep out on the glaciers which would have to be done if either of these two peaks was attempted. Wills then suggested the Wetterhorn. 'Ja, ja, Herr', Lauener answered immediately. He added that no one had ever succeeded in climbing it, although he almost certainly knew that this was not true. It was a guide's job to keep his client happy.

The Wetterhorn lies in the central Bernese Alps, the Oberland, eastwards of the village of Grindelwald, one of the places from which it can be climbed. It consists of three peaks: The Hasle-Jungfrau (3,690.8m) which, strangely enough, although it is the second highest peak, is the principal Wetterhorn ascent; the Mittelhorn (3,708m) and the Rosenhorn (3,681m). All three Wetterhorn peaks had been climbed long before Wills appeared on the scene; but he was probably genuinely ignorant of the fact until later.

The Rosenhorn had been climbed by Edouard Desor, the first German to climb a first-class peak, together with two guides from the Grimsel (the Pass and Hospice to the south east of it), M. Bannholzer and Johann Jaun, a member of a famous guiding family, on 28 August 1844.

Three days later these two guides went on to climb the Hasle-Jungfrau for the first time. Desor also made the first ascent of the Lauteraarhorn (4,042m) which lies south of the Wetterhorn group.

Wills' party arrived at Grindelwald on the morning of 16 September 1854 and there Lauener asked Wills' permission to engage one more guide. Wills agreed, though with some reluctance because of the expense. He already had three guides and one porter.

The man chosen by Lauener was Peter Bohren of Grindelwald. He was only 5ft tall; but he had already been on an attempt on the Wetterhorn (Hasle-Jungfrau) in July 1845

with a party which may or may not have reached the summit; and he had been one of two guides on what in all probability was a successful attempt by Eardley J. Blackwell on 14 June 1854 when they had planted an 'iron flag' just short of the summit. He was a fine climber who was given the nickname, *der Gletscher-Wolf*.

At 1.30 pm on 16 September 1854, Wills, Balmat and the porter set off from the inn at Grindelwald, leaving Mrs Wills and her brother to await the outcome of the climb. 'Samson' had already spent a considerable time assuring her that he would answer with his life for that of her husband's, 'which made us all laugh,' as Wills wrote in *Wanderings Among the High Alps*: but this good work was largely undone by the innkeeper who expressed himself in a more gloomy fashion. 'Try', he said, 'to return all of you alive.' What subsequently transpired seems to show that he was probably more worried about not being paid for the miserable provisions he had supplied for the climb.

The other two members of the expedition, Lauener, who was the leader, and Bohren, started later. They had been delayed by the non-delivery of what they described as a '*Flagge*', which to Wills' mystification they had ordered not from a seamstress but from the village blacksmith.

As they moved across the green meadows on the northern slopes of the Grindelwald Valley in the hot sunshine Wills could contemplate the three gigantic mountains which rise above its south side: the Eiger, the Mettenberg, which forms the base of the Schreckhorn, and the Wetterhorn.

After an hour of this leisurely progression they reached a châlet near the foot of the upper glacier, where Bohren's father lived, 'with a number of his almost numberless progeny, all of whom came forth, and with much interest bid their brother [who had just caught them up] and ourselves, God speed.'

Their route now took them up the Enge, a narrow zig-zag path along the edge of a rock wall, Bohren 'smoking like a chimney pot' on the way, until they reached the point where it changed direction to the eastwards (away from Grindlewald) where they waited on a grassy platform for Lauener to come up.

When he did it was with the '*Flagge*'. This consisted of a sheet of iron, 3ft by 2ft, supported by a bar of solid iron, 10–12ft long, the whole fantastic construction weighing between 20–30lb. The Chamonix men, by nature much less frivolous than the Ober-landers, described it as *une bêtise*, a nonsense.

From this point, immediately above the upper Grindelwald Glacier, they moved up over slippery limestone to a promontory around which it poured on its way down the mountain side from the Wetterhorn Plateau. From here they descended to the foot of the valley, which Wills described as being hidden from the spectator in the Grindelwald Valley by an intervening ridge, where a number of streams poured out of it over a lip of rock. One of these streams formed a rainbow, 'A glory placed there by the Eternal Hand', as Wills put it. They now ascended this valley towards the foot of the glacier which descends from the summit ridge of the Hasle-Jungfrau, and to Wills the precipices at the head of the valley below the glacier appeared to be unclimbable.

After climbing this valley for about half an hour they came to a sort of cave, formed by three boulders. It stood on the banks of a torrent from the glacier and here, at about 8 pm, they halted for the night, although Wills felt that they should have made the ascent to the glacier that evening.

There they ate a not very exciting meal provided by the innkeeper: 'a hunch' of cold veal, 'a log' of sour bread and some black coffee, heated over a fire, the fuel for which they had lugged up the mountain. Then they turned in on the earth floor which had been strewn with straw by some previous occu-pants.

As soon as the candle was blown out the Oberlanders began to sing a German hymn. Wills did not join in. What followed was a

night of horror: the noise made by the torrent was deafening, the interior of the hut was stiflingly hot, the blankets full of fleas and 'the cold veal seemed to rise up in judgement upon me'. At 2 am, almost mad with thirst he forced his way out of the cave which the guides had hermetically sealed with rocks for a refreshing draught followed by a glacial bath in the torrent.

They left at 4.30 am, too late for Wills' liking, without the porter for whom there was no longer any need, and climbed up through the terminal moraine of the glacier, a difficult thing to do by the light of a lantern.

Day had already broken when they reached the lower end of the glacier and it took them an hour to get from it to the foot of the rock wall below the upper ice plateau, which had looked so difficult from the valley and looked almost as bad close-to. In reaching it they only encountered one crevasse on the glacier.

Here, standing out from a nearly perpen-dicular wall of rock were a series of thin parallel wedges ... planted with the thin edge upwards, at right angles to the body of the mountain, and separated from one another by deep intervening clefts and hollows. Each of these was two or three hundred feet in height, seventy or eighty in width at the base, but narrowing off to the thickness of a few inches, and present-ing, at the top, a rough and jagged ridge, forty or fifty feet long, by which one must pass, to reach the plateau beyond.

They proceeded to climb one of these wedges and then, with Lauener leading and a rope stretched along it as an aid to balance, they made their way along the crumbling crest, dislodging pieces as they went, 'some as large as a leg of mutton', as Wills described them, his mind very much on food, which fell away to the depths below. All this was accomplished while lugging the great '*Flagge*' and its post.

Beyond this crest they found themselves

The last rocks before the summit and (*right*) the arrival at the summit. Drawings by Mrs Wills (*Alpine Club*)

on the edge of the upper ice plateau and from it looked down the precipice to the Grindelwald Valley and the village. Here they rested for a short while on a pile of débris and ate some breakfast. Again Wills was out of luck, all the meat was heavily flavoured with garlic and he had to make do with wine mixed with snow and a crust of bread. Bread and wine was to be his staple diet for the rest of this strenuous day.

Here, at the edge of the plateau, they cached all their gear, except for their alpenstocks and axes, some rope and a flask of brandy.

Wills noted how much more effective the alpenstocks used by the Oberland men were than those still in use at Chamonix which were nothing but long, iron-shod poles. In fact these Oberland alpenstocks were very similar to some ice-axes still in use today. The Oberlanders also had proper crampons, whereas Wills and the Chamonix men preferred the local type, double-headed metal points screwed into the soles of their boots.

They now roped up and commenced to climb a steep slope through thick snow, close in to a steep ridge which linked the Mittelhorn with the Wetterhorn. They were now on the far, eastern, side of the summit from Grindelwald.

It took them an hour to gain about a thousand vertical feet, following a zig-zag route and cutting steps in the snow which overlaid the ice and which became progressively thinner as they ascended. At the end of that time, at about 10 am, they reached the upper part of the plateau where they rested by some dark crags. The weather was perfect. While they were sitting there, unroped, two other climbers came into view, one of them carrying a young fir tree, and to the surprise of Wills' party they now proceeded to take the lead. They turned out to be two chamois-hunters who had decided that an all-Oberland party should also go to the summit and in order to reach it at the same time as Wills' they had climbed the lower part of the mountain during the night.

The two men were Christian Almer and his brother-in-law, Ulrich Kaufmann. While Kaufmann became a famous guide, Christian Almer was soon to become perhaps the greatest of all the early Alpine guides, with the possible exception of Melchior Anderegg of Meiringen, and he was to climb with some of the best climbers of the period (such men as A. W. Moore, the Reverend Hornby and his partner, the Reverend Philpott, the Reverend W. A. B. Coolidge, Leslie Stephen and Whymper). Almer's favourite peak was always to be the Wetterhorn and in 1896, the year of their golden wedding anniversary, when he was seventy years old and his wife was seventy-one, they both climbed it, and he himself climbed it again the following year.

A shouting match now developed between the two parties and tempers rose high. Balmat, normally a mild man, even threatened to deliver some 'coups de poing'. Soon, however, it was realised that Almer and Kaufmann had no intention of stealing a march on Wills' party, the whole thing was amicably arranged, the two newcomers became 'bons enfants', as Balmat put it, and the two parties continued to climb the mountain together, with Almer and Kaufmann bringing up the rear.

What they now had to overcome was a very steep ice face, some 600ft high, which led up to an enormous, overhanging ice- and snow-cornice which effectively blocked the view of what lay beyond. This slope was covered with a coating of loose snow, only 2–3in thick, too thin for making steps which had to be cut through into the ice beneath.

Up this very exposed slope Lauener led the way, cutting steps on a zig-zag course, followed by Samson whose job it was to enlarge them. They did this while the others waited below, dodging as best they could the chunks of ice dislodged by the Oberlanders' ice-axes which whizzed past them over the ridge and down the precipices below. Eventually, Wills was hit on the back of the head by one of these chunks; but when he

suggested to Balmat that the leaders should make longer traverses between each zig-zag which would have the effect of diverting some of the debris further to one side and also help to prevent the steps already cut being filled with falling snow, Balmat said in a slightly reproving tone: 'Mais où tomberaient-ils, monsieur, si, par un malheur, ils glissaient? A présent, il y aurait la chance que nous pourrions les aider; mais si on glissait à côté-voilà, monsieur!' ('But what if they should fall, monsieur, if, by bad luck, they slipped? At the moment there would be a chance that we could help them, but if anyone slipped over to that side . . .'). He pointed to a block of ice which passed, a little to one side, and bounded into the frightful gulf.

It took the two men an hour to reach the foot of the cornice and then the rest of the party climbed up to it, clearing the snow out of the steps as they went. With the aid of his alpenstock, which he stuck in the ice vertically, Wills calculated that the angle was about 45 degrees at the foot and between 60 and 70 degrees beneath the cornice, which 'curled over towards us, like the crest of a wave, breaking at regular intervals along the line into pendants and inverted pinnacles of ice, many of which hung down to the full length of a tall man's height.'

At this point Lauener, taking a stance at right angles to the cornice, gave it a succession of thwacks with his axe, bringing down a large chunk of the cornice which fell to the foot of the slope and over the arête.

Suddenly [Wills wrote] a startling cry of surprise and triumph rang through the air. A great block of ice bounded from the top of the parapet, and before it had well lighted on the glacier [the ice slope] Lauener exclaimed, 'Ich schaue den blauen Himmel!' ['I see blue sky!']

In a few minutes Lauener and Samson had enlarged the breach and soon the entire party was able to pass through it, literally onto the summit of the Wetterhorn, which was nothing

49

but a ridge 4in wide, overlaid by cornices. It was 11.20 am.

> The instant before [he wrote] I had been face to face with a blank wall of ice. One step, and the eye took in a boundless expanse of crag and glacier, peak and precipices, mountain and valley, lake and plain. . . . The next moment I was appalled by the awfulness of our position. The side we had come up was steep; but it was a gentle slope compared with that which now fell away from where I stood. A few yards of glittering ice at our feet, and then, nothing between us and the green slopes of Grindelwald, nine thousand feet beneath. . . . Balmat told me repeatedly afterwards, that it was the most awful and startling moment he had known in the course of his long mountain experience. We felt as in the more immediate presence of Him who had reared this tremendous pinnacle, and beneath the 'majestical roof' of whose deep blue heaven we stood, poised as it seemed, half way between earth and sky.

After giving rein to these very natural sentiments—an epitome of a sense of what Victorian climbers felt about the mountains in their relation to God—Wills and his companions were glad to straddle this knife-edge which the indefatigable Lauener and Samson now exposed with their axes for a distance of about ten feet.

Sitting in this uncomfortable but reasonably secure position, wearing white flannel trousers, Wills now took off his hat and waved it to the watchers at the telescopes in the valley. They failed to record this courtesy but had already remarked, according to Wills, the mystery of there being more men at the summit than had set off on the expedition. This suggests that the inhabitants of Grindelwald knew nothing of the attempt that was being made by Almer and Kaufmann, which in a small, peasant community, seems almost unbelievable.

Almer, Kaufmann and Bohren now began to utter a series of uncouth cries; but they were soon checked by Balmat with the words, 'No shouting at the summit! You never know what might happen,' which instantly silenced them.

All of Wills' party, including Wills himself, now took a part in setting up the iron '*Flagge*' which was only attached to the iron flagpost after it had been driven into the ice to a depth of about six feet. At the same time Almer and Kaufmann set up their pine tree, which looked even more odd, apparently growing from the ice. While this was going on Balmat noticed that another iron '*Flagge*' was flying from a similar iron pole to their own, embedded a few feet below the ridge on which they sat astride. This had been erected three months previously by Blackwell, Christian Bleurer and Peter Bohren who was on the present expedition. Blackwell and Bohren must have been as quiet as the grave about their participation but Wills' own account is nevertheless mystifying: 'We knew that the

Ulrich Kaufmann, former chamois hunter and well known early Alpine guide. He and his brother-in-law, Christian Almer, joined Wills' party (uninvited) on the successful ascent of the Wetterhorn. (*Alpine Club*)

ascent had been attempted that year by a gentleman whose flag still floated over the more attainable peak of the Mittelhorn, but no better comment could be devised on the reality and greatness of the difficulty we had overcome in passing the cornice.'

At 11.40 am, twenty minutes after they reached the summit, they began the descent. 'Now we are in our Lord's hands!', Samson exclaimed, for which he was rebuked by Balmat who told him that nothing should be said that would make the descent appear worse than it was actually likely to be.

The descent of the ice-curtain below the cornice was made unroped—against Wills' advice, on the grounds that if one of the party fell, all would be carried away which, at that time before the technique of belaying had been evolved, was very probable—and it naturally proved a memorable experience for Wills. When they were 45m down the ice-slope, someone remembered that they had forgotten to drink the health of the Wetterhorn while at the summit, proof if any was needed of the profound effect that being at the top had had on guides and amateur alike, and this act of primitive magic was effected on the ice there and then, each member of the party drinking, bareheaded, a draught of brandy mixed with snow.

At 12.15 pm they reached the black crags, from which they had watched Lauener and Samson cutting the way to the cornice. At 12.45 pm they reached the point on the edge of the upper ice-plateau where they had left their gear and provisions; and there they had a meal, Wills confining himself to bread, being still unable to stomach the meat flavoured with garlic; but drinking a toast to the Wetterhorn with his companions, and their two new-found friends, in iced red wine, accompanied by 'as loud a shout as human lungs could utter'.

At the foot of the wedges they glissaded down the scree and Wills proved so expert at this that any doubts the guides had felt previously about his ability to reach the valley that evening were dispelled. The same

technique was employed on the glacier, where Lauener was so alarmed at his employer's zest that he tried to hold him back above a crevasse spanned by a snow and ice bridge, with the result that they both took a tumble. At 2.45 pm they reached the cave where they found the porter who, rather than descend by himself, as had been arranged, had preferred to await their return.

There they drank a bottle of champagne and, after walling up the cave to keep it dry for future climbers, they went on down the mountain. They made a triumphal entry into Grindelwald, each man with his hat decorated with red berries, which Lauener had insisted they should pluck for this purpose while descending the Enge.

Both Balmat and Samson decided that Mont Blanc was '*une bagatelle*' compared with the Wetterhorn which put all the local Oberlanders in high good humour and Wills was left with a perfectly enormous bill for four guides at 50 francs each, a porter at 15 francs and a monstrous bill for the rather

Ulrich Lauener, one of four brothers, all famous guides. It was Ulrich, a 'huge bearded fellow', who made a breach in the ice cornice with his axe through which the party passed to the summit (*Alpine Club*)

The Bernese Alps. On the horizon from left to right: Wetterhorn, Lauteraarhorn, Schreckhorn, Finsteraarhorn, the Greater Fiescherhorn, Eiger, Mönch and Jungfrau (*Swiss Tourist Office*)

miserable provisions provided by the innkeeper, amounting to 60 francs, which he successfully disputed. The whole thing cost him nearly £10, which was a lot of money in those days.

Nevertheless it was worth it; and whatever the rights and wrongs, and whoever really was the first man to reach the summit of the Wetterhorn, we may safely leave to those who have made a study of the subject. What is certain is that this had been a day to remember.

7 Ascent of the Matterhorn

By the summer of 1865, the last summer of the Golden Age, almost the only true great Alpine peak still unclimbed was the Matterhorn (4,477m) on the Swiss-Italian border. A huge and solitary monolith, it rises 1,500m clear above the glaciers which lap it on four sides, more than 2,700m above the village of Zermatt on the Swiss side below the North-East Ridge; and more than 2,100m above what was, in 1865, the small hamlet of Breuil on the Italian side below the South-West Face. The Italians know it as Monte Cervino, and the French as Mont Cervin. It is one of the most outstanding mountains in the entire world.

The North-East or Hörnli Ridge is the longest of all. The next ridge to it, in a clockwise direction, is the South-East Ridge, the most difficult, which runs down to the Furgggrat. The Furgggrat Ridge separates the Furgg Glacier, which is wholly in Switzerland, from the Cervino and Forca Glaciers to the west, in Italy. These two ridges, the Hörnli and the South-East Ridge, enclose the colossal East Face of the mountain which falls away to the Furgg Glacier and looks very much as though someone had been attempting, not very successfully, to smooth it with a trowel.

The next face, the South-West Face, the one seen from Breuil in the Valtournanche, is enclosed between the South-East and South-Western Ridges, and is in Italy. It is made up of a series of huge precipices and snow-couloirs.

The South-West, or Italian, Ridge descends from the Italian Summit which is 1.1m lower than the Swiss Summit at the northern end of the ridge, to what is known as the Shoulder, the Épaule which, as its name implies, forms an almost horizontal section below the summit pyramid. The Shoulder terminates in Peak Tyndall and from this the Italian Ridge descends by way of the Cravate, the Crête du Coq and the Great Tower to the Lion Arête, the lowest point of which is the Col du Lion. It then rises again to the Tête du Lion, a small peak to the west. This South-West Ridge was the scene of the earliest attempts to climb the mountain.

The next ridge is the magnificent North-West, or Zmutt, Ridge. The upper part consists of slabs but it becomes increasingly jagged before sweeping down as a snow-covered ridge towards the Zmutt Glacier at the head of the Zmutt Valley west of Zermatt.

Between the Lion Arête of the South-West Ridge and the Zmutt Ridge the great West, or North-West, Face of the Matterhorn overhangs the Tiefenmatten Glacier in Swiss territory; and, finally, between the Zmutt Ridge and the Hörnli Ridge are what Whymper referred to as 'the ghastly precipices' of the North Face impossible even to contemplate climbing in the early days.

The North Face is an Alpine Grade VI climb with a great deal of loose rock and stone constantly falling from above, and it was not successfully accomplished until July 1931, when the brothers Franz and Toni Schmid arrived at Zermatt from Munich, on their bicycles, and reached the summit, after bivouacking on the face in two sleeping bags attached to it by pitons.

The first known reconnaissance of the mountain was made from Breuil on the Italian side in the midsummer of 1857. The party consisted of Jean-Antoine Carrel, a

View from Hörnli Ridge, the towers of Furggen Ridge in the background beyond the eastern face. 'We were now fairly upon the mountain and were astonished to find that places which, from the Riffel, or even from the Furggengletscher, looked entirely impracticable, were so easy that we could run about'—Whymper (*John Cleare*)

twenty-eight year old stonemason who had served with the Piedmontese Army and fought against the Austrians in 1849—his nickname was 'Il Bersagliere', after the famous regiment; Jean-Jacques Carrel, Jean-Antoine's uncle, a tough chamois-hunter, between forty and fifty years old, and Aimé Gorret, a seminarist, described by Guido Rey, the urbane Italian author of the definitive work on the earlier attempts on the mountain, himself a great guideless climber, as 'a beardless lad of about twenty, something between a cleric and a shepherd'. All three were inhabitants of the Valtournanche. They were encouraged to make the attempt by Canon Carrel of Aosta, a kinsman of the Carrel's who realised that if they succeeded tourists would flock to what was a miserably poor region.

They left the Chalets d'Avouil, in the meadows above Breuil, while the stars could still be seen, taking with them some food, a hatchet, which Jean-Jacques Carrel kept secreted inside his shirt, and three *grafios*, ash-plants with a hook at one end, used for pulling marmots from their holes.

They reached the Col de Tournanche at a height of 3,484m and from it looked down on to the Tiefenmatten Glacier, 500m below, in Switzerland. 'Their wonder was great', Rey wrote, 'when they found ... a valley completely covered with ice and enclosed by rocks of enormous height. They stood there for a moment speechless, almost terrified at the sight of its savage beauty; it was so different from their native valley.'

On this occasion they reached the Tête du Lion, west of the Col du Lion, at a height of about 3,657m. The following year the two Carrels are thought to have reached the base of the Great Tower at about 3,840m.

In the summer of 1860, twenty year old Edward Whymper, the man who in five years time was to become the best known climber in the world, appeared at Zermatt, not as a climber, but as an artist—by profession he was a wood engraver. This was the year that the Parker brothers, climbing with-out guides, reached about 3,500m on the East Face and Professor Tyndall and his guide Bennen reached a height of about 3,860m on the Great Tower.

Whymper's original ambition was not to climb mountains—inspired by the search for Franklin he wanted to become at Arctic explorer.

In 1861 he made his first serious climb, the first ascent by a British climber of Mont Pelvoux (3,946m) in the Dauphiné. It was now that Whymper conceived the idea of climbing the Weisshorn, one of the few remaining major peaks in the Alps still unscaled; but in August news reached him that Professor Tyndall, with the guides Bennen and Wenger, had succeeded in climbing it and that the Professor was already at Breuil, preparing for his second attack on the Matterhorn. Whymper, who still referred to himself as 'a novice', determined at least to attempt to forestall him.

At the foot of the Valtournanche, Whymper engaged an unnamed Swiss guide from the Oberland, and on the way to Breuil learned that 'Jean-Antoine Carrel of the village of Valtournanche, was the cock of the valley.'

Carrel would only go with him for a fee of 20 francs a day and on condition that he also hired Jean-Jacques Carrel. Whymper agreed to the fee, but demurred at the sight of the chamois-hunter who had what he described as 'an evil countenance' which was hard on Jean-Jacques who was a rough but ready fellow.

When Whymper and his guide arrived at Breuil on 28 August, Whymper learned that the Professor and Bennen had made a close inspection of the mountain and that Bennen had given his opinion that it was 'difficult and dangerous and that it was impossible to reach the summit from Breuil in a single day'.

Whymper now decided to attempt the South-West Ridge with his Oberland guide who had no experience of the mountain. On the 29 August 1861 they ascended to the highest cowsheds on the way to the Col du

North Face of the Matterhorn. The Hörnli Ridge is on the left, the Zmutt Ridge on the right and beyond it, in shadow, is the Italian Ridge (*John Cleare*)

The Matterhorn from the south-west during a big westerly storm. The point reached by Professor Tyndall, on his second attempt, is the Enjambée, close to the point where the shoulder on the right joins the foot of the final peak (*Bradford Washburn*)

Lion and while they were there Jean-Antoine and Jean-Jacques Carrel also arrived, Jean-Antoine having no intention of seeing the mountain, on which they had expended such efforts, succumb to a young arrogant foreigner eleven years his junior, and a foreign guide. In spite of their rivalry the four men spent the rest of the night together, tormented by the fleas, and the following morning the Carrels left before dawn, whereas Whymper made a leisurely departure around 7 am. 'I admired their pluck,' Whymper wrote,

'and had a strong inclination to engage the pair; but finally decided against it . . .'

That day Whymper and his guide climbed to the Col du Lion, where they could hear the Carrels high above them. They then went down to get their tent and pitched it on the edge of the precipice above the Tiefenmatten Glacier.

The tent was unsatisfactory. It was a new model designed by Francis Galton, the foremost authority of the day on travel and exploration. It 'opened like a book . . . the

flaps of the tent would not keep down, the pegs would not stay in, and it exhibited so marked a desire to go to the top of the Dent Blanche, that we thought it prudent to take it down and sit upon it.'

Meanwhile, the Carrels had succeeded in climbing the Chimney (the Cheminée), above the Col du Lion, which, although swept by falling stones, was free of ice. The highest point reached by Whymper was the foot of the Chimney where he had a quarrel with his guide whom he called a coward.

Beyond this *mauvais pas* the Carrels climbed another 91m to what is known as the Crête du Coq, at an altitude of about 3,962m, the highest point so far reached. There, Jean-Antoine cut the date, a cross, his initials and a design of a tiara on the rocks with the spike of his ice-axe. While descending, Jean-Jacques lost one of his shoes and glissaded down the Couloir du Lion with his foot done up in a handkerchief.

Whymper lists nine attempts to reach the summit of the Matterhorn in the course of the next four years. In 1862 he himself made more than one attempt from the Breuil side with R. J. S. Macdonald, various guides, and with a little hunchback, Luc Meynet, who carried the tents; but they only reached the ridge below the Chimney, 30m above the Col. On another occasion the same year Whymper set out alone and succeeded in reaching what is known as the Cravate, a prominent patch of snow at a height of 4,041m. On the way down he fell 'nearly 60m in seven or eight bounds', wounding himself in twenty places, most seriously in the head, although he managed to apply a chunk of snow to stop the bleeding before losing consciousness—when he eventually reached Breuil his appearance caused consternation. In 1863 he made his sixth attempt, this time with the two Carrels and a couple of porters, equipped with two 12ft, jointed ladders, having brought them through the Italian customs by saying that he was an acrobat! They reached the Crête du Coq (about 4,047m) still far short of the highest point reached by Tyndall in 1862—the Enjambée, a chasm separating the Shoulder from the summit pyramid.

In 1863 the Italian Alpine Club was founded at Turin by a number of leading climbers, among them Quintino Sella, the great statesman of the Risorgimento, and Felice Giordano, both of whom were also scientists. Monte Viso (3,841m), the Piedmontese peak in the Cottian Alps had been climbed two years previously by a party led by W. Mathews and Giordano and Sella were both determined that the first party to reach the top of the Matterhorn must be Italian. They sent the young Italian writer and politician, Giuseppe Torelli, to Breuil to enlist Carrel. He agreed and the following year (1864) Giordano met him and it was decided that an attempt should be made in 1865.

Whymper arrived at Breuil in June 1865. On the 21st he made an attempt on the South-East Face by way of the Breuiljoch, a pass he had prospected on a reconnaissance in 1863, which crossed the Furgggrat Ridge between the Cervino and the Furgg Glaciers.

Equipment used by Whymper in 1865, now in the Alpine Museum, Zermatt (*Swiss Tourist Office*)

With him were Michel Croz, Christian Almer of Grindelwald who had climbed the Wetterhorn with Wills, and Franz Biner. That year all four men had together made the ascent of the Dent Blanche (4,357m), at the head of the Val d'Hérens, and of Point Whymper, the 4,184m western summit of the Grandes Jorasses in the Mont Blanc group. With them as porter was Luc Meynet. At 10 am they were at the foot of 'a noble couloir, which led straight up into the heart of the mountain for fully a thousand feet . . . then bent towards the north, and ran up to the rest of the south-eastern ridge.' There, Whymper records, he saw a few small stones falling

Almer was seated on a rock, carving large slices from a leg of mutton, the others were chatting, and the first intimation they had of danger was from a sudden roar—which reverberated awfully amongst the cliffs, and looking up they saw masses of rocks,

boulders and stones, big and little, dart round the corner eight hundred feet or so above us, fly with fearful fury against the opposite cliffs, rebound from them against the walls on our side, and descend; . . . some bounding down in leaps of a hundred feet or more over the snow; . . . The precious mutton was pitched on one side, the winebag was let fall, and its contents gushed out from the unclosed neck, whilst all four cowered under defending rocks, endeavouring to make themselves as small as possible . . .

Such a panic I have never witnessed, before or since, upon a mountainside

This attempt was abandoned at a height of about 2,413m, and an attempt to cross the Furggjoch, a crossing parallel to the Breuil-joch, for an attempt via the Hörnli Ridge with this strong team came to nothing.

On 7 July he arrived at Breuil with Christian Almer and Franz Biner. There he found that Carrel had made another un-

The scene of Whymper's fall of 'nearly sixty metres in seven or eight bounds' on the Italian Ridge, wounding himself most seriously in the head but applied a chunk of snow to stop the bleeding before losing consciousness (*Mansell Collection*)

A storm at midnight 10 August 1863, by Whymper. His tent can be seen at the top of the snow-capped ridge (*Alpine Club*)

successful attempt on the Matterhorn with César Carrel, the Abbé Gorret and J. J. Maquignaz, but had been driven back by bad weather. Both Almer and Biner refused to attempt it—'*Anything* but Matterhorn, dear Sir!' Almer said, '*anything* but Matterhorn'. Croz had had to go to Chamonix to meet an English client. The only hope was Carrel.

Whymper's plan was to cross the Théodule Pass by moonlight on the night of 9 July, pitch a tent high up on the East Face above the Furgg Glacier on 10 July, and make the attack on the 11th. Carrel only agreed on condition that if the attempt failed Whymper would revert to the Italian route by way of the South-West Ridge. Whymper thereupon discharged Almer and Biner—'with much regret, for no two men ever served me more faithfully or more willingly. ... During the preceding eighteen days (I exclude Sundays and other non-working days) we ascended more than 100,000ft, and descended 98,000ft.'

On 8 July Whymper was busy preparing for the climb; the weather was bad. On the morning of 9 July he set off at his habitual five miles an hour to visit the devotee of guideless climbing, the Reverend A. G. Girdlestone, who was lying ill at Valtournanche. On his way there he met a gentleman ascending the valley with a mule, baggage porters and Jean-Antoine and César Carrel. This, although Whymper did not know it, was Giordano who had now, inopportunely for Whymper, arrived for the Italian attempt on the mountain.

Jean-Antoine lied to Whymper, telling him that they were just helping the other party on its way, but that, in any event, neither he nor César would be able to serve Whymper after 11 July as they had been engaged to travel 'with a family of distinction'. Whymper, justifiably annoyed, asked Carrel why he had not told him of this engagement when he had agreed to climb with him. 'Because,' said Carrel, 'it was not settled. The engagement is of long standing, but *the day* was not fixed. When I got back to Valtournanche on Friday night, after leaving you, I found a letter naming the day.'

On the morning of the 11th a party of seven guides, including César, and led by Jean-Antoine, set off to climb the mountain from the Châlets d'Avouil where they had concealed their climbing equipment so that Whymper would not get wind of their intention. The guides were to blaze the way and then Giordano and Sella would be led to the summit.

Whymper was in a difficult situation. He had dismissed his guides and all the capable local men were on the mountain. Even the gallant Meynet was unable to accompany him as his cheese-making activities were at a critical point. However, all was not yet lost. The mountain was shrouded in mist and Carrel had to find a way to the summit before he could take up Giordano and Sella. During this time Whymper could reach Zermatt and make an attack by the East Face and the Hörnli Ridge. If this failed he could probably get back to Breuil in time to 'start at the same time as the Messieurs, and yet

get to the top before them'.

By good fortune, at midday on the 11th, a party arrived at Breuil from Zermatt by way of the Théodule Pass, 'preceded by a nimble young Englishman and one of old Peter Taugwalder's sons'. This was Lord Francis Douglas, the eighteen-year old son of the 7th Marquis of Queensberry who, although only on his third season in the Alps, had made a number of first ascents. He brought news that Peter Taugwalder the elder considered that the mountain might be climbed by the Hörnli Ridge. He himself had come to Breuil to enlist Carrel and he now asked Whymper if he could take part in his expedition.

At Zermatt they engaged the elder Peter Taugwalder and there, to Whymper's astonishment, he found Michel Croz, sitting on the wall outside the Monte Rosa Hotel. Croz had met his client at Chamonix, but he had been forced to return to England, and Croz was now about to set off with the Reverend Charles Hudson for an attack on the Matterhorn. Hudson, aged thirty-seven, was an extremely tough individual—according to Whymper he could average 50 miles a day in his prime—and had made a number of guideless climbs, including a winter attempt on the Aiguille du Goûter while reconnoitring a route to the summit of Mont Blanc in 1853. He had also made a number of first ascents, including the first guideless and first ever ascent of Mont Blanc from St Gervais in the Val Montjoie, and a first ascent of Mont Blanc by the Bosses Ridge in 1859. Hudson had with him a friend, Douglas Hadow. Hadow, who was nineteen and on his first season in the Alps, had only made two minor ascents, during that summer, and a short and sharp ascent of Mont Blanc—from the Grands Mulets to the summit in under four and a half hours and from the summit to Chamonix in five—being a snow mountain this had little in common with the Matterhorn.

Whymper and Douglas now asked Hudson to join forces with them, on the grounds that 'it was undesirable that two independent parties should be on the mountain at the same time with the same object'. Hudson agreed.

'Before admitting his friend, Mr Hadow,' Whymper wrote, 'I took the precaution to inquire what he had done in the Alps, and, as well as I can remember, Mr Hudson's reply was, "Mr Hadow has done Mont Blanc in less time than most men".'

'He [Hudson] then mentioned several other excursions that were unknown to me, and added, in answer to a further question, "I consider he is a sufficiently good man to go with us." Hadow was admitted without any further question.' It was an error of judgement on Whymper's part. Anxious to secure the services of his old guide, Croz, he accepted what, in his heart, he must have known to be wrong.

The morning of 13 July was fine without a cloud in the sky. At 5.30 am the over-large and ill-assorted party set out from Zermatt. It consisted of Whymper, Hudson, Lord Francis, Hadow, Croz, Peter Taugwalder and his two sons, Peter and Joseph, who were to act

Whymper's illustration of the 'cannonade' he experienced in 1862 under the South-West Ridge (*Alpine Club*)

as porters. The leader was Croz. At the Schwarzsee Chapel they picked up the rope which had been left there: 'There were three kinds,' Whymper wrote. 'First, 200ft of the Manilla rope; second, 150ft of a stouter, and probably stronger rope than the first; and a third, more than 200ft of a lighter and weaker rope than the first, of a kind that I used formerly (stout sash line).' It was this sash line that was in use during the fatal descent from the mountain.

From the foot of the Hörnli Ridge, at 11.30 am, they moved onto the East Face. 'We were now fairly upon the mountain,' Whymper wrote, 'and were astonished to find that places which from the Riffel, or even from the Furggengletscher, looked entirely impracticable, were so easy that we could *run about*.' By noon they were at a height of 3,352m and there constructed a platform for the tent, while Croz and young Peter Taugwalder went ahead to reconnoitre. At 3 pm they returned with the news that the whole party could reach the summit in a single day. The weather was still perfect, so perfect that only Whymper, Lord Francis Douglas and the Taugwalders slept in the tent. The following morning, before dawn, they began

to climb, leaving Joseph Taugwalder to return to Zermatt, and now the whole of the slope revealed itself, in Whymper's words, 'rising for 3,000ft like a huge natural staircase. ... For the greater part of the way there was, indeed, no occasion for the rope, and sometimes Hudson led, sometimes myself.'

By 9.55, after one halt for about half an hour, they were at the Shoulder (4,267m) and at this point halted for fifty minutes. For the most part they kept clear of the North-East Ridge which was full of rotten rock. 'We had now arrived at the foot of the part which, from the Riffelberg or from Zermatt, seems perpendicular or overhanging and could no longer continue upon the eastern side', Whymper wrote, and now roped, with Croz leading, Whymper second, then Hudson and Peter Taugwalder, followed by Hadow and old Peter Taugwalder, they crossed the Hörnli Ridge to its northern side above the Matterhorn Glacier and continued to climb what was no more than a 40-degree slope over rocks covered with a thin film of ice.

'Mr Hadow was not accustomed to this kind of work, and required continual assistance. It is only fair to say that the difficulty

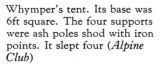

Whymper's tent. Its base was 6ft square. The four supports were ash poles shod with iron points. It slept four (*Alpine Club*)

which he found at this part arose simply and entirely from want of experience.'

Croz led them on this traverse of the North Face for a distance of about 130m, then vertically up it for about 20m before turning to the left to re-join the ridge. From it 'a long stride round a rather awkward corner brought us to snow once more. The last doubt vanished! The Matterhorn was ours! Nothing but 200ft of easy snow remained to be surmounted!'

Fearful that the Italians might forestall them at the last moment Whymper and Croz began a race to the summit, as soon as the slope became sufficiently easy and arrived on it at precisely the same moment, 1.40 pm. They were on the true summit of the Matterhorn, on the Swiss side of the border, at a height currently accepted to be 4,777.5m, and there were no footprints, proof on such a fine day that Carrel's party had not reached it.

But, Whymper immediately thought, what about the Italian Summit beyond the border, connected to the Swiss Summit by a ridge some 80m long, and about a metre lower? Whymper hastened across the dip to the Italian Summit, followed by Croz. There were no footprints there either.

'I peered over the cliff,' Whymper wrote, 'half doubting, half expectant, and saw them immediately—mere dots on the ridge [the South-West Ridge close to the Cravate, according to Whymper who interrogated Carrel later] and *twelve hundred and fifty feet* below us.' In fact they were almost certainly much higher, on the Shoulder 150–180m below the summit. Both men shouted to attract the attention of the Italians, but apparently to no avail.

'We drove our sticks in, and prized away the crags,' Whymper wrote, 'and soon a torrent of stones poured down the cliffs. There was no doubt about it this time. The Italians turned and fled.'

Although they were not launched with malevolence their effect is scarcely surprising. Men unthinking enough to throw down stones from the top of a mountain are a menace.

Down at Breuil, Whymper's party were seen by Giordano who mistook them for the Italians. He immediately despatched a triumphant letter to Sella. Carrel had completely underestimated the ease with which the East Face and the North-East Ridge could be climbed, as had everyone else, Whymper included.

What had happened on the Italian side was that the second party had set up their tent at some 4,200m at the foot of the Great Tower, where they were pinned down by bad weather. However, they do seem to have wasted a considerable amount of time on the day Whymper's party set off from Zermatt, which was exceptionally fine. On the 14th, Carrel's party did not begin to climb until 6 am and, at 2 pm, when they saw Whymper's party on the Italian Summit, they were still on the Shoulder. Having done so, to Giordano's consternation, they turned back, arriving at Breuil half-dead, early on the morning of the 15th.

He [Carrel] did not understand to what extent he could have shared in the triumph [Guido Rey wrote] if he had continued, whatever the cost, if he had gained the summit a few hours after his rival, having, by so doing, solved the problem of the ascent of the Matterhorn by the Italian face ... that would certainly have been a much more difficult victory than the Englishman's.

On the summit Croz now planted a tent pole in the snow to which he attached his blouse as a flag—it was seen by watchers at Breuil, who believed that it was set up by Carrel's party, at Zermatt, and at the Riffelberg, the mountain above it.

The party spent an hour on the summit, during which time they built a cairn. Then, all the climbers, except young Peter Taugwalder, and Whymper, who had been asked at the last moment to write the names of the party and leave them in a bottle, began to move down the mountain on the route by

The first to climb the Matterhorn. The four in the upper row fell to their death on the descent (*Alpine Club*)

MICHEL A. CROZ.

Hadow.

Charles Hudson 1828-1865

Lord F. Douglas 1847-65

Peter Taugwalder-Vater

Edward Whymper 1865

1865 (22)
Peter Taugwalder Sohn

which they had climbed it. Whymper, according to himself, had already suggested to Hudson that a fixed rope should be set up at the difficult part where they had gone over from the East to the North Face, about 80m below the summit, and Hudson approved. Whymper then tied himself to Peter Taug-walder and the two of them ran down the easy snow-slope to catch up the others who were just beginning the descent of this difficult patch. It was now nearly 3 pm. The order in which the climbers were descending was first Croz, followed by Hadow, Hudson, Lord Francis Douglas and old Peter Taugwalder. 'Great care was being taken', Whymper wrote. 'Only one man was moving at a time;

when he was firmly planted the next advanced and so on. They had not, however, attached the additional rope to rocks, and nothing was said about it.' At about 3 pm Lord Francis asked Whymper to tie on behind old Peter Taugwalder as he was afraid that Taugwalder would not be able to maintain his position in the event of a slip by one of the others. Whymper and young Peter were now roped to the rest of the party.

A few minutes later a boy in Zermatt saw what he told Seiler, the landlord of the Monte Rosa Hotel, was an avalanche from the summit down the North Face. At that moment Croz, Hadow and Hudson were close together. Hadow slipped and Croz, who had turned to help him plant his feet, having put down his ice-axe, was thrown off his balance:

I heard one startled exclamation from Croz, [Whymper wrote] then saw him and Mr Hadow flying downwards; in another moment Hudson was dragged from his steps, and Lord F. Douglas immediately after him. All this was the work of a moment. . . . Immediately we heard Croz's exclamation, old Peter and I planted ourselves as firmly as the rocks would permit: the rope was taut between us, and the jerk came on both of us as one man. We held; but the rope broke midway between Taugwalder and Lord Francis Douglas. For a few seconds we saw our unfortunate companions sliding downwards on their backs, and spreading out their hands, endeavouring to save themselves. They passed from our sight uninjured, disappeared one by one, and fell from precipice to precipice on to the Matter-horngletscher below, a distance of nearly 4,000ft in height. From the moment the rope broke it was impossible to help them.

So perished our comrades. For the space of half-an hour we remained on the spot without moving a single step. The two men (old and young Peter Taugwalder) paralysed by terror, cried like infants, and trembled in such a manner as to threaten us with the fate of the others. . . .

According to Whymper, roped between the two Taugwalders, he was unable to move until young Peter was finally persuaded to do so—'The father's fear was natural he trem-bled for his son; the young man's fear was cowardly—he thought of self alone.'

When all three were at last standing to-gether Whymper discovered that the broken rope was the sash line, the oldest and weakest of the three.

At 6 pm they reached the shoulder of the Hörnli Ridge, where they were out of danger and there they witnessed a 'Brocken Spectre',

a natural phenomenon of the mountains. It was in the form of a mighty arch and it was doubly awe-inspiring in the circumstances.

The following morning, after a bivouac on the ridge, they reached Zermatt. 'Seiler met me at the door,' Whymper wrote, 'and followed in silence to my room. "What is the matter?" "The Taugwalders and I have returned." He did not need more and burst into tears; but lost no time in useless lamen-tations, and set to work to rouse the village.'

The bodies were found the next day, Sunday, on the plateau at the high part of the Matterhorn Glacier. Their boots had been torn off and were lying on the snow. Hadow's were seen to be in a deplorable condition for such a climb. 'They had fallen below as they had fallen above—Croz a little in advance, Hadow near him, and Hudson some distance behind; but of Lord Francis Douglas we could see nothing (a pair of gloves, a belt, and one of his boots were found). We left them where they fell; buried in snow at the base of the grandest cliff of the most majestic mountain of the Alps.' Three days later the bodies were brought down and buried in the churchyard at Zermatt.

It is unnecessary to go at great length into the subsequent melancholy story of accusa-tions and counter-accusations, which princi-pally centred on the ludicrous suggestion that old Peter Taugwalder cut the rope. Whymper disposed of this suggestion so thoroughly that it is scarcely worth a mention. The ropes taken up from the Schwarzsee were all Whymper's and it was primarily his responsi-bility to ensure that the sash line was not used except for the purpose for which it was in-tended, though both Croz and old Taug-walder were at fault for not having seen that the proper ropes were being used.

Meanwhile on the Breuil side of the Matter-horn, a fresh attempt began on 16 July. It was made by Jean-Antoine Carrel, Aimé Gorret, now an Abbé, who had been on one of the original attempts in 1857, Jean-Baptiste Bich, and Jean-Augustin Meynet, both in the employ of the innkeeper at Breuil.

It was Gorret who pushed the others into going with the words 'So you give up the Matterhorn! You do not want to go again. I will go myself. Who will follow me?' At 1 pm they reached the foot of the Great Tower where they pitched their tent. The weather was perfect.

After an uneventful night they made coffee and at daybreak on the morning of the 17th began the gelid ascent of the Great Tower, —the morning sun does not reach the South-West Ridge until much later than the Hörnli Ridge. They then ascended past the Crête du Coq and the Cravate until, at 10 am on the 17th, using a fixed rope left by Tyndall in 1862, they reached the Enjambée, the moat which separates the Shoulder from the summit pyramid, and the crossing of which must have been accomplished by descending and crossing at a lower level.

They were then brought to a halt by the steep cliffs down which Whymper and Croz had hurled rocks, and Carrel traversed the Shoulder onto the North-West Face above the Tiefenmatten Glacier, where they were exposed to falling stones and icicles, some of which, according to Whymper, attained a length of 30m on this upper part of the mountain. Eventually they reached a fault in the face resembling a gallery along which they edged towards the Zmutt Ridge.

At the end of this gallery, a couloir too wide for them to negotiate separated them from the ridge and it was the Abbé, the biggest and strongest man—his nickname at Breuil was the Mountain Bear—who gallantly renounced the opportunity to stand on the summit of the Matterhorn and lowered Carrel and Bich into the abyss, so that they might cross it.

Around 3 pm Carrel and Bich reached the Italian Summit and from there went on to the Swiss Summit where they planted a flag beside the cairn erected by Whymper's party, and noted the disturbed snow on the Matterhorn Glacier where the English party had fallen. They then descended the North-West Ridge to the point where the Abbé was waiting beyond the couloir. By 9 pm they were back at their camp at the foot of the Great Tower. It was not until their return to Breuil, where they were fêted, that they heard of the disaster.

Once the Matterhorn was climbed Whymper seldom climbed in the Alps. Thereafter he travelled widely: to Greenland, in 1867 and 1872, to the Andes with the Carrels in 1879 and 1880, where he climbed Chimborazo, Sincholagua, Antisana and Cotopaxi and several other peaks, to the Canadian Rockies with the guide Christian Klucker of Sils in 1901 and again in 1904 and 1909 when he made a large number of first ascents. Although he largely abandoned the Alps as a climber, Whymper continued to visit Zermatt and Chamonix.

It is rare in the history of human endeavour, particularly in mountaineering, for anyone to have found fame in disaster and to have capitalised on it so successfully as this lonely, friendless man.

Thirty-four year-old Walter Bonatti, the Italian guide who accomplished the first solo climb of the North Face of the Matterhorn in 1965 in winter. He spent four days and three nights on the sheer face in temperatures down to — 22°F (*Central Press*)

8 William Augustus Brevoort Coolidge and Dog Tschingel

One of the greatest climbers of his time, and, indeed, the whole Victorian age, was an American, the Reverend William Augustus Brevoort Coolidge. Born near New York in 1850, a distant cousin of the American President, he was a sickly, short-sighted and precocious child. He took Holy Orders in 1882 after becoming a fellow of Magdalen at Oxford, in 1875. For thirteen years he acted as honorary curate at South Hinksey in Oxfordshire but, as the *Dictionary of National Biography* put it, 'He chose a manner of life which made it for long intervals difficult to perform clerical functions.'

Coolidge was the first of his compatriots to become truly famous in the Alps, although James Kent Stone of Boston, later Father Fidelis, preceded him in time, having made the first ascent of the Blümlisalphorn with Leslie Stephen as early as 1860, as well as ascents of Monte Rosa, the Lysjoch and the Strahlhorn, to name only some of his climbs. Scarcely anyone, in fact, has equalled Coolidge's assiduity as a climber—the list of his climbs covers twenty-two pages of *The Alpine Club Register*. It begins with his ascent of the Niesen (2,362m) in the Bernese Alps, which he climbed in 1865 with his aunt, Miss Meta Brevoort, who taught him to climb, and ends with an ascent of the Ortler (3,899m)—then in Austria now in Italy—in 1898, when he was forty-eight.

Not only was Coolidge an outstanding climber, a fact belied by his rather rotund appearance, he was also by far the most prolific chronicler of climbs, mountaineering history and topography. By 1912, by his own computation, he had produced 220 articles, entries in encyclopedias and other books, and his contributions to the famous Conway and Coolidge Climbers' *Guides*, the first of their kind, were particularly valuable.

Coolidge was almost incredibly meticulous —on one occasion he dismissed an important and scholarly book because an accent had been printed on 'Besançon'. Sent a copy of one of his own books for review by an editor who had been unable to find anyone else competent to review it, he proceeded to search his own text for errors with such minute care that he was able to detect a number worthy of correction. For such reasons Coolidge did not lack enemies and it is this almost Teutonic thoroughness which makes some of his writing almost unreadable except by the most devoted admirers and those who know the climbs he describes.

When his father died, and his mother became an invalid, his upbringing was largely entrusted to his mother's sister, Miss Meta Brevoort, herself a remarkable climber, and, from 1865 onwards until her death in 1876, William and his aunt spent almost all their time in Europe, not missing one season of climbing. Miss Brevoort was an extraordinary character in an age of characters. She was not exactly a fast mover, as she nearly always insisted on climbing in the heavy women's clothes of the period. She was not beautiful; but neither was she ugly and she did not deserve the description that one writer left of her as '*eine grosse Holländische-Amerikanische Miss*'. She used to beat donkey drivers who ill-treated their animals, was an ardent republican—she sang the Marseillaise on top of Mont Blanc as an insult to the Emperor Napoleon and then danced a quadrille with her guides. And she was tough

The Reverend William Augustus Brevoort Coolidge, born in New York, fellow of Magdalen, Oxford in 1875, curate at South Hinksey, Oxon and the first American to become truly famous in the Alps. He was brought up largely by his aunt, Miss Meta Brevoort, herself a remarkable climber. She sang the Marseillaise on the top of Mont Blanc as an insult to the Emperor Napoleon (*Alpine Club*)

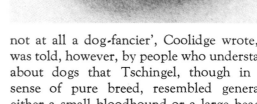
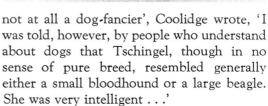

—one had to be to put up with Alpine living conditions in those days.

It was in 1868 that Miss Brevoort and William first met Christian Almer. 'He can't speak a word of either English or French,' she wrote to her sister, 'so we have a fine chance of improving our German . . . he . . . sensibly remarked that he could soon tell after a day's walk with us what and how we could go. He is a short little man with an honest intelligent face, and very communicative.'

The walk must have been satisfactory because Miss Brevoort was able to engage him for a month, and on 8 July they climbed the Wetterhorn together. Three days later they set off from the Kleine Scheidegg Pass for an attack on the Eiger, but unfortunately the rocks were so heavily glazed with ice that it had to be abandoned, much to William's disappointment. He was now just eighteen and in his fourth Alpine season. To cheer him up Almer gave him his dog, a bitch named Tschingel. By this time she had already mothered thirty-eight puppies. 'I am

not at all a dog-fancier', Coolidge wrote, 'I was told, however, by people who understand about dogs that Tschingel, though in no sense of pure breed, resembled generally either a small bloodhound or a large beagle. She was very intelligent . . .'

Tschingel could understand Swiss-German and soon learned English, but resolutely refused to learn French. She greatly enjoyed red wine, and warm, weak tea: 'after revelling in this drink she would retire to a corner, sit down, and utter piercing howls—apparently of excessive and overwhelming pleasure, just as when she heard music. . . . She was also a great pursuer, whenever she sighted or scented them, of chamois, marmots, hares and foxes.'

What distinguished Tschingel, however, from most other intelligent mongrels was that she was a passionate mountaineer and invariably climbed under her own steam. Almer had bought her for 10 francs in 1865 and that year she trotted up the steep snow slope to the summit of the Torrenthorn which was her first known ascent. She then embarked on a notable career, which included the crossing of the (2,316m) Gemmi pass, in company with Almer and a great Golden Age climber, the Reverend Hereford Brooke George—the first advocate of rucksacks and ice-axes to replace uncomfortable knapsacks and long alpenstocks.

Tschingel's first big climb with her new owners was on 18 July 1868, when she reached the top of the Blümlisalphorn (3,664m). On the steep, final slope to the summit she had a fall, but was caught by her collar before plunging down to the Oeschinen See. 'She seemed to like it very much', Coolidge wrote of her climb, 'and, so we thought, the panoramas from tops, running on ahead of us to the summit of a peak, and then running back to encourage us by showing how near we were to the wished-for goal.'

That year, among other peaks and passes, she climbed the Balmhorn (3,701m), descending by the Zagen Pass (3,042m) to Leukerbad; the Aletschhorn (4,195m), on which expedition Coolidge recalled, 'my aunt went up the Sparrhorn to look at us, and we waved Tschingel in the air as a sort of red flag', and she also conquered the Gross Nesthorn (3,820m). Her last pass that year was the Mönchjoch, a pass of over 3,352m. In the course of crossing it she was let down the face of a glacier on a rope. 'On glaciers', Coolidge wrote, 'she was always roped (coming immediately after my aunt), the rope passing through a ring on her work-a-day collar.'

What suffered most, as with most climbers at high altitudes, were her feet and her owners endeavoured to make things easier for her by having leather boots made to measure, but Tschingel disliked them and invariably kicked them off.

In July 1871 she climbed the Jungfrau, meeting the great Hungarian climber, de Déchy, who was greatly surprised to see her. September 1872 was her great month. She climbed the Finsteraarhorn (4,275m), on the 5th, three times crossed the Grünhornlücke

Christian Almer, guide and friend of Miss Brevoort and the Reverend Coolidge to whom he gave Tschingel in 1868 (*Alpine Club*)

(3,305m), the third time ascending to the Agassizjoch (3,750m). On the 11th she climbed the Hasle Jungfrau peak of the Wetterhorn (3,703m) and, on the 18th, the Gross Doldenhorn (3,650m), by which time she had accomplished all but three of the great peaks in the Bernese Oberland (the Bietschhorn, the Gross Schreckhorn and the Gross Fiescherhorn).

Her subsequent feats are too numerous even to summarise. Her highest ascents were the Breithorn (4,171m) and Monte Rosa in 1875 (her nose peeled a bit). After this triumph, some English climbers at the Riffel, which commands fantastic views of numerous peaks, including the Matterhorn and the Breithorn, elected her an Honorary Lady Member of the Alpine Club.

Here, we must take leave of what Miss Brevoort always called 'the dear hund'. Altogether, by the time she retired from active climbing in 1876 after her last climb with Miss Brevoort, the highest peak of the Fusshörner (3,628m), she had, in her eleven-year career, climbed thirty peaks and crossed thirty-six passes, a total of sixty-six.

It was the last climbing season for Miss Brevoort as well as for Tschingel for she died three months later. Coolidge continued to climb with Christian Almer until 1884 and after that date with his son, also Christian Almer. From 1880 to 1889 he was editor of the *Alpine Journal*, becoming increasingly irascible and stubborn. In 1897 he left his home in Oxford for Grindelwald, where he lived until his death in 1926.

Tschingel died in Dorking, Surrey, in 1879, by which time she was quite blind. Coolidge had attempted on several occasions to steel himself to have her put down and when he finally made the decision she anticipated him by dying in her sleep.

Tschingel, first canine Alpinist, understood Swiss-German, learned English but refused to pick up French although she enjoyed red wine (*Alpine Club*)

THE EIGER

9 The North-West Face

The Eiger is one of the great Bernese Oberland peaks which loom over the Grindelwald Valley on its southern side. From some angles it looks like a tooth, and on the side facing the valley it falls away to the meadows of Kleine Scheidegg as a 1,828m precipice. This is the Eigerwand, the North Face of the mountain and the greatest mural precipice in the Alps. Black, in perpetual shadow, unlovely, a vast concave triangle of limestone hung with snowfields, often obscured by mist and clouds, battered by violent storms, wracked by frost and swept by avalanches of snow and rotten rock, the Eigerwand is, in a word, repellent, and it has been the scene of some of the most desperate climbs ever made.

The first ascent of the mountain (3,970m) was made by way of the West Ridge and the West Face, the only easy route, in 1858. The climbers were Charles Barrington and the guides Christian Almer and Peter Bohren of Grindelwald.

Of the other two principal ridges of the Eiger, the South and North-East Ridges, the South Ridge joins up with the Mönch (4,099m, 13,463ft), adjoining the Eiger by way of the Eigerjoch, a saddle between the Eiger and the Mönch.

The other ridge, the long North-East, or Mittellegi, Ridge, although descended by Moritz von Kuffner, a wealthy Viennese, together with three guides, in 1885, was not climbed until 1921 when a very young Japanese climber, Yuko Maki—later, in 1956, to lead a successful Japanese attempt on Manaslu (8,156m) in the Nepal Himalaya—climbed it with three guides from Grindelwald, Fritz Amatter, Samuel Brawand and Fritz Steuri the elder. They are said to have used a long pole to negotiate some parts of the route.

The North-East Face of the Eiger which overlooks the Grindelwald Valley, loosely known as the North Face, is separated from the Eigerwand by the North Buttress and the summit was reached by way of this face and the buttress in 1932, in a classical piece of climbing, without pitons, by a party of great Swiss climbers, Dr Hans Lauper and Alfred Zürcher and the Valaisian guides Josef Knubel and Alexander Graven, two of the finest climbers of their time—Lauper had already climbed the North Faces of the Mönch and Jungfrau. This was the first climb of the North-East Face and the route, which the climbers described as very difficult but interesting, is known as the Lauper Route.

The first attempt on the Eigerwand was made in August 1935 by Max Sedlmayer and Karl Mehringer, two young Bavarians. They set off at 2 am on 21 August and were last seen climbing the sheer-smooth ice of the Third Ice-Field five days later, after a night of gales and extreme cold. Nearly four weeks later one of them was spotted by a pilot who succeeded in flying close to the wall: he was knee-deep in snow, frozen to death at what must have been their last bivouac on the upper edge of the Third Ice-Field, at the top of the ridge known as the Flat-iron.

The next attack on the Wall was made in the summer of 1936 by two German and two Austrian climbers and ended in one of the great tragedies of Alpine history. This was the year of the Olympic Games at Berlin and Hitler announced that the first team which succeeded in climbing the Wall would be

The North Face of the Eiger
(*John Cleare*)

awarded gold medals—the whole enterprise, in which gallantry to the point of extreme foolhardiness was displayed, was clouded with misplaced patriotism and a demonic urge to enhance the reputation of National-Socialism.

The two Austrians, Willi Angerer and Edi Rainer, both good rock-climbers, were joined by the Bavarians, Andreas Hinterstoisser and Toni Kurz, a qualified guide from Berchtesgaden and, like Hinterstoisser, a member of a German mountain regiment.

By making a very difficult diagonal traverse below an unclimbable crag, the Rote Fluh, across to the first of the three ice-fields on the Face, Hinterstoisser discovered the secret of climbing the lower part of the Wall, but having done so he made retreat impossible by retrieving the rope.

On the third day they reached a point just below the Death Bivouac of Sedlmayer and Mehringer and there they were seen to turn back. All four climbers were last seen the following day, 21 July, when the weather worsened, and Hinterstoisser was trying to set up his traverse in reverse. He failed and fell to his death, unroped, probably trying to insert a piton to take an *abseil* rope. At the same time, Angerer who had already suffered a fractured skull from falling stones higher up the Wall also fell and was strangled by the rope, while Rainer was hauled up close to a karabiner by it and was frozen to the face.

The only survivor was Kurz, left swinging across the face in a rope sling, midway between the two corpses, with the rescue party which had climbed out through one of the embrasures of the Jungfrau Railway which winds up through the face, unable to reach him. By the following morning, having hung there throughout a night of storm his left arm was frozen solid. In spite of this Kurz, invisible from the rescue party because of an overhang, was able to obey their instructions to lower himself down the face, cut away the rope from Angerer's body, climb up to Rainer's and cut the rope there, thus giving himself two lengths of rope. These he

The team—four Germans and a Scot—who scaled the North Face by the direct route in 1966 for the first time, battling through blizzards in sub-zero temperatures: (*left to right*) Jörg Lehne, Günther Strobel, Roland Votteler, Dougal Haston, Siegi Hupfauer (*Chris Bonington*)

unplaited, using one hand and his teeth, and then joined the strands together to make a single rope to which the rescue party attached the materials for an *abseil*. This took him between five and six hours.

The *abseil* rope was about 3m too short and another had to be knotted to it. It was this fatal knot which jammed in the kara-biner which clipped his sling to the rope on which he was descending. And there he died an ice-axe length from his would-be rescuers, with the last words, spoken very clearly, 'I'm finished'.

The first successful attack was made in July 1938 by an Austro-German party. The Germans were Ludwig Vörg who had already reached the Death Bivouac the previous year with Matthias Rebitsch, and Andreas Heckmair. The Austrians were Heinrich Harrer and Fritz Kasparek, and these two set off on 21 July, the second anniversary of Hinterstoisser's desperate attempt to make his return traverse.

Like the German team which followed

them, they were greatly helped by the rope which Vörg and Rebitsch had set up on the Traverse the previous year, especially as the face was glazed with ice. Without it they might not have been able to make the traverse and at the Swallow's Nest, at the upper end of the Traverse, a point also used by Vörg and Rebitsch, they left some equipment for a possible retreat, including 100m of rope. The weather was fine.

By early afternoon they had reached the foot of the Second Ice-Field, which had taken Rebitsch and Vörg five hours to cross the previous year; but instead of doing so they traversed diagonally to a projecting rock above the upper part of the Rote Fluh, and there they bivouacked, tying themselves to pitons and passing an uncomfortable night.

The morning of the following day, 22 July, was very difficult for Harrer who was without crampons and it was Kasparek who cut a staircase for him on their diagonal climb of the Second Ice-Field and it was just below the rock wall which separates the Second

Three routes up the Eiger. Charles Barrington's way up in 1858 was by the West Ridge and the West Face on the right, ('Had I not been as fit as my old horse, Sir Robert Peel, when I won the Irish Grand National with him, I would not have seen half the course.'); the others are the modern routes (*John Cleare*)

from the Third Ice-Field that Harrer looked back down the staircase: 'Up it I saw the New Era coming at express speed; there were two men running—and I mean running, not climbing up it. ... It hardly seemed possible that they had only started ... today.'

These were Vörg and Heckmair, wearing the latest twelve-point crampons and from this point they agreed to climb together. It was now about 11 am.

By 2 pm they had reached the Death Bivouac and mist began to shroud the Wall as it often does in the afternoon. Now they traversed a 60-degree ice-slope to the Ramp, an enormous chimney of smooth rock with few hand holds or cracks to take a piton. In it, while the two parties were on separate ropes, Kasparek came off and fell 18m through the air. Fortunately the rope by which Harrer had him belayed ran over a snow ridge which cushioned the shock and he was unscathed.

On this night of 22 July they bivouacked together in the upper part of the Ramp where it began to narrow, one party 2m above the other, Harrer and Kasparek hanging from the rock on one thin, square-shafted piton—what Harrer called 'our little grey steely friend'. 'The relaxed attitude of Vörg, the "Bivouac King", was quite remarkable' Harrer wrote, 'even in a place like this he had no intention of doing without every possible comfort. He even put on his soft fleece-lined bivouac slippers, and the expression on his face was that of a genuine connoisseur of such matters.'

That night Harrer slipped off his perch in his sleep and when he awoke found that he was hanging on the rope over the void.

On the morning of 23 July, after a hot breakfast of porridge and coffee Heckmair led the difficult last part of the chimney which was full of ice, bringing them out at the foot of a hideous bulge of ice at least 10m high, covered with icicles, which was again successfully pioneered by Heckmair.

I had never seen a pitch that looked so hazardous, dangerous and utterly extraordinary, Harrer wrote, . . . Vörg had a tight hold on the rope, ready at any moment to hold Heckmair if he came off . . . But he didn't come off. We couldn't imagine how, but in some masterly fashion or other he managed to drive an ice-piton deep into the ice above the bulge and thread the rope through a snap-link. Then he gave the order: 'Pull!' Vörg pulled him up on the rope, over the bulge, up to the piton.

They now traversed out to the right, all roped together, under an overhang which protected them from stone-falls and avalanches and at the end of it Heckmair led the way out up a 30m crack, an extremely difficult climb over ice-glazed rock which he accomplished wearing crampons.

By the time they emerged, an awe-inspiring thunder storm was brewing and by the time they had negotiated the long, horizontal, rock traverse, later named the Traverse of the Gods because of its splendour,

to the Spider, snow was falling accompanied by thunder and lightning.

The Spider is a huge field of ice set here in the near vertical face, so called because it channels out over the Wall in innumerable long narrow cracks and gullies. The upper gullies have the unpleasant capacity of collecting snow and ice falling from above which then sweeps out over the body of the Spider removing anyone who happens to be in its path; and it was here that just such an avalanche swept over Harrer and Kasparek, at that moment fortunately belayed to ice-pitons.

The other two were not belayed. They were on a sort of rocky island over which the ice debris swirled hip deep, but Heckmair was able to drive in his ice-axe and grab Vörg who was below him by the collar, preventing him from being swept away.

Slowly it grew lighter. [Heckmair wrote] and the pressure ceased. We knew then, but could scarcely believe, that we had

Iced beer and beards on the Eiger: Günter Strobel, first up in 1966 has his first beer for over a month; (*right*) Jörg Lehne was the second up (*Central Press*)

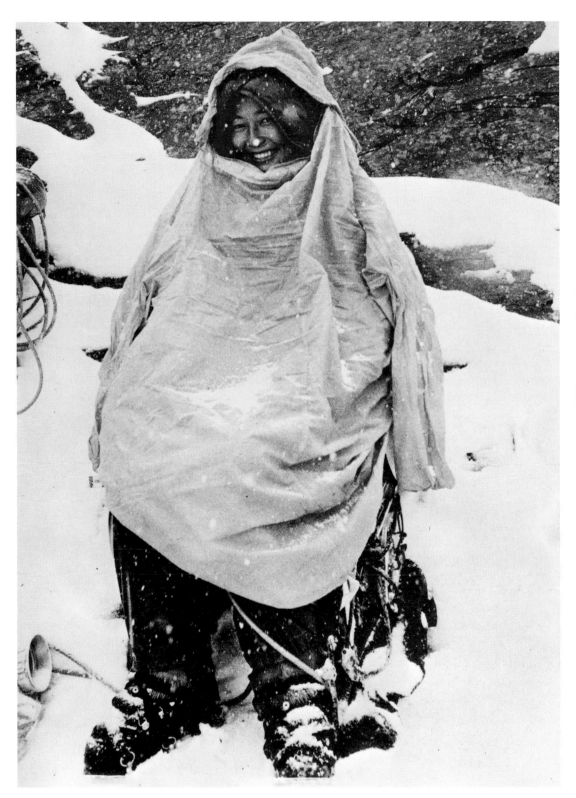

Miss Michiko Imai, 27 year-old doctor, the only woman member of a six-strong Japanese climbing party who conquered the North Face by the direct route in August 1969. She acted as medical officer when one of her companions fell 20m, breaking his nose (*Central Press*)

North Face March 1968:
Bonington and Haston (*lower*)
(*John Cleare*)

(*Far right*) Dougal Haston on
the North Face, 1968 (*John
Cleare*)

come through safely ... 'Wiggerl' [Ludwig] I cried. 'They're still on!'

It seemed impossible, an outright miracle. We started to shout, and there they were, actually answering. An indescribable joy swept over us. One only discovers how strong a thing team-spirit can be when one sees the friends again whom one has counted as dead.

The last bivouac was on a narrow projection of rock above the Spider. Again they were pitoned to the rock but this time 10ft apart, so that they had to use a traversing rope with a karabiner attached to share a cook pot of coffee—the only thing they could face—which Vörg went on brewing interminably. The only member of the party who was not altogether happy was Kasparek who had cut one of his hands badly on the Spider and all of whose cigarettes were wet.

The next morning it was snowing and the whole Wall was white, but they decided to continue and, after a meal of coffee and melted chocolate in condensed milk, they set off, all four roped together with Heckmair leading, as they had agreed he should, for the summit. Before doing so they jettisoned some food, a symbolic act in such circumstances.

Heckmair was now leading, followed by Vörg, Harrer and Kasparek who was made last man so that he would not have to overhaul the rope with his badly injured hand.

The last part of the climb was made at a furious, dangerous speed, because of the avalanches which were sweeping the face. At one point Heckmair came off, but was literally caught by Vörg whose hand was deeply pierced through his gauntlet by his friend's crampons.

Just then a little phial of heart drops came to hand in the first-aid bag. That devoted woman Dr Belart of Grindelwald had made me take it along in case of emergency, remarking: 'If Toni Kurz had only had them along, he might even have survived *his* ordeal. . . .' On the bottle it said 'ten drops'.

I simply poured half of it into Wiggerl's mouth and drank the rest, as I happened to be thirsty.

After many hours of climbing, of furious 'chasing and racing', as Harrer put it, always in snow and with visibility a few metres, they heard shouts from above—these eman-ated from two Austrian climbers, Rudi Fraissl and Leo Brankowsky, and a party led by the guide Hans Schlunegger, all of whom had climbed the Eiger by the North-West Face, alarmed by the fearful weather, to see if they could carry out a rescue operation. In order to prevent them from embarking on such a hazardous operation, and because they did not need help, they did not reply and the would-be rescuers went down to the valley filled with gloom.

The last part was up an interminable snow-slope in the teeth of a howling blizzard. So dark was it that Heckmair and Vörg, with their heads down, narrowly missed walking clean over the summit and falling down the South Face.

At 3.30 pm on 24 July, all four men stood on the summit. By this time Harrer and Kasparek had been eighty-five hours on the Wall, Heckmair and Vörg sixty-one hours. That evening they reached Kleine Scheidegg, in pouring rain. Their route became known as the Original or 1938 Route.

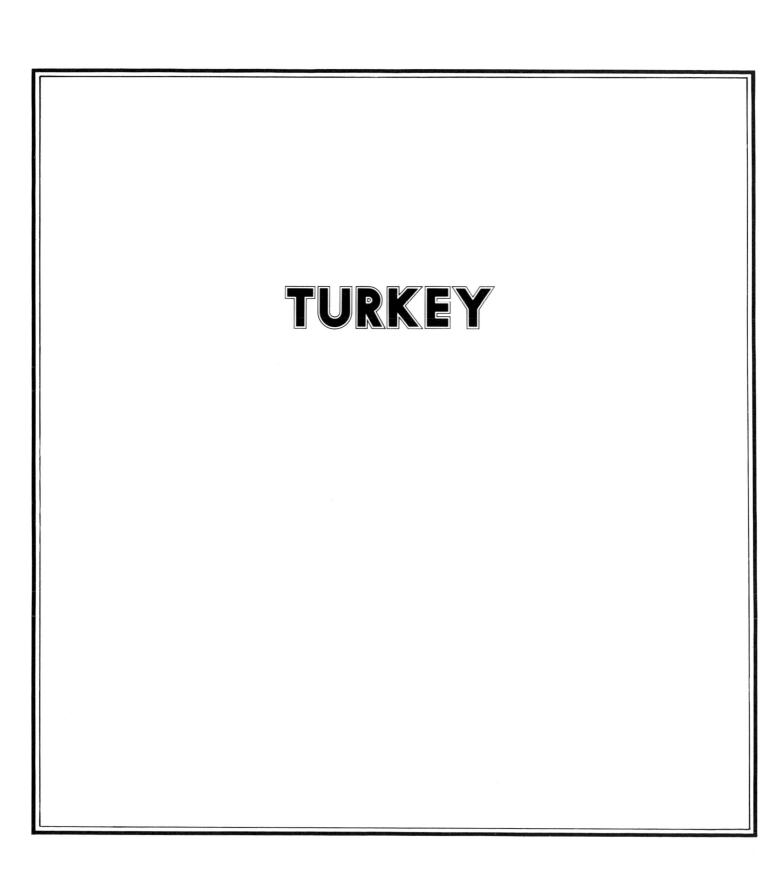

TURKEY

10 Mount Ararat

'The earliest mountain ascent of which any record has been preserved is the ascent of Mount Ararat by the patriarch Noah,' Francis Gribble wrote in his fascinating book, *The Early Mountaineers* (1899). 'It was accomplished in a combination of circumstances which is extremely unlikely to recur.'

Ararat was, and still is, venerated as the scene of the delivery from the Deluge, although most Muslims and some Christians believe Mount Gudi or Judi in Southern Kurdistan is the correct site having once been covered by a convent said to house fragments of the Ark.

The mountain consists of Great Ararat (5,156m) and Little Ararat (3,914m) to the south east, linked by a saddle more than 2,400m high. Until the later part of the nineteenth century Little Ararat formed the trijunction of the Russian and Turkish empires with the Persian dominions of the Shah, while the saddle marked the frontier between Russia and Turkey. As a result, the slopes of Little Ararat became a convenient place of refuge for banditti, principally Persians and Kurds.

Apart from a saddle to the north west of Great Ararat, which links it to a range of volcanic mountains running westwards between the upper waters of the Aras and the Eastern Euphrates, the whole Ararat massif rises in splendid isolation from the Armenian Plateau—Great Ararat looms almost 4,300m above the plain of the Aras to the north, slightly less in the south above the plain of Bayazit and the main road from Turkey to Iran, and is easily visible from a hundred miles away. Bryce, one of the early climbers to reach the summit, wrote: 'The noble thing about Ararat is not the parts but the whole. I know nothing so sublime as the general aspect of this huge yet graceful mass seen from the surrounding plains. . . .'

In 1254 the Flemish Franciscan traveller, William of Rubruck, on his way back to Europe from the court of the Great Khan Mangu at Karakorum in Mongolia, passed close under Great Ararat and noted that the Ark rested on the higher summit, whence an angel had brought down a piece of it to a monk who lodged it in a church nearby as a holy relic. Eighteen years later, in 1272, Marco Polo passed through Armenia on the way to the court of the Great Khan at Cambaluc (Peking). He did not see it, but left an accurate account, '. . . the snow never melts' [on the summit], he wrote, 'and is constantly added to by new falls. Below, however, the snow does melt, and runs down, producing such rich and abundant pasture from a long way about, and it never fails them. The melting snow also causes a great amount of mud.'

Apart from Noah, who was presumably engaged in an extremely hazardous descent accompanied by a vast menagerie, the only other known climber in the early years of the Christian era was St Hagop (Jacob), an Armenian monk. He made several attempts to climb the mountain in order to venerate the Ark which, at that time, apparently could still be seen, perched on the summit, from the foot of the mountain in clear weather. On the third attempt an angel appeared to him bearing the news that God had forbidden anyone to climb the mountain and as a consolation he gave Jacob a fragment of the Ark, which he subsequently deposited in a monastery near Yerevan, now the capital of

Soviet Armenia. The belief that no one could reach 'the secret top' of Ararat persisted at least until the end of the nineteenth century and may still do so among certain Armenians.

The first recorded ascent was not made until October 1829 when Dr Frederick Parrot, a Russo-German professor at the University of Dorpat in Estonia, reached the summit on his third attempt, accompanied by three Armenians and two Russian soldiers. Parrot used the same route as St Hagop as far as the monastery. From there he climbed in a westerly direction to the Kip Ghöll, a small lake on a plateau at a height of about 4,000m and from there by snow-slopes and terraces to the twin summits of Great Ararat. Parrot was an experienced mountaineer. He had already made the first ascent of the Parrot-spitze (4,336m), the fifth highest summit of Monte Rosa, as well as an unsuccessful attempt on Kazbek (5,047m), in the Central Caucasus, in 1811, the mountain to which, according to legend, Prometheus was chained and which was not climbed until Freshfield

reached the top with a party in 1868.

In *Journey to Ararat*, the English translation of his book *Reise zum Ararat* (Berlin, 1834), Parrot wrote that the top of Great Ararat which had intrigued geographers and theologians for so long, was,

a gently vaulted, nearly cruciform surface, of about 200 paces in circuit, which at the margin sloped off precipitously on every side, but particularly towards the S.E. and N.E. Formed of eternal ice, without rock or stone to interrupt its continuity, it was the austere silvery head of Old Ararat.

After spending three-quarters of an hour on the summit, where there was no sign of the Ark, making observations and suffering considerably from the intense cold, he took his party down to St Jacob's Monastery on the edge of the valley of Ahiru, the Great Chasm which runs deep into the north-east side of the mountain. Yet, in spite of Dr Parrot's undoubted probity and seriousness, and the testimony of his Russian soldiers, no one in

Great and Little Ararat from the north-east from James Bryce's *Transcaucasia and Ararat*. Bryce, jurist, historian, politician and one-time British ambassador in Washington reached the summit in 1876. He found a piece of shaped wood well above the treeline which proved not to be part of the Ark but only left behind by a Russian surveying party (*Alpine Club*)

the neighbourhood believed that he had reached the top. In fact two of his Armenians, possibly at the suggestion of the Church authorities, testified that, although they had ascended to a considerable height, there were still peaks above them. What was worse, he was also disbelieved by a number of Russian savants and he died before subsequent climbers were able to corroborate what he had written.

In the 1840s further ascents were made, notably by a German naturalist, Dr Wagner, in 1843. He was probably the first European to record an earthquake of cataclysmic proportions which happened on the mountain in 1840. It destroyed 6,000 houses in what was a lightly populated region, and in the habitations on the mountain's slopes. According to eye witnesses, half an hour before sunset, a violent earth tremor of about two seconds' duration was followed by an immense explosion and a rush of air from the head of the Great Chasm. This produced a vast rent in the mountain side and huge

quantities of mud and rocks weighing upwards of fifty tons were ejected into the air. Of some 2,000 people only 114 survived. Four days later 'thousands and thousands of tons of water', produced by the masses of snow and ice and the torrential rain, burst through the huge fall of stone and clay which was damming the Great Chasm and roared down the valley in one final act of destruction, covering the plain of Aras with mud and boulders.

Another German, an eminent geologist, Herman Abich, reached the summit in 1845 and, in 1850, a Russian party under the command of General Chodzko, spent three days encamped on the summit. They were engaged on a triangulation survey of Caucasia and Trans-Caucasia which resulted in a splendid series of maps on a scale of five versts (Russian measure equalling approx. $\frac{2}{3}$ mile) to the inch. They had started out from below the ridge linking Great and Little Ararat, as did two British soldiers, Major Stuart and Colonel Monteith who, having

been assured by the local people that the mountain was unclimbable, considered that theirs was the first ascent!

The climb that is perhaps most interesting, simply because he described it so well, was made in the autumn of 1876 by James Bryce, jurist, historian, politician, the author of *The American Commonwealth* and one-time British Ambassador in Washington. Also, he climbed the last 1,500m alone and found a piece of shaped wood far above the treeline not part of the Ark, but left behind by General Chodzko's surveying party.

Bryce and Aeneas Mackay, another legal and historical writer, set off from St Petersburg to Moscow, thence down the Volga to the Caspian Sea and eventually arrived in Armenia. They reached a height of 2,286m at Sardar Bulakh, and pressed on to 3,352m. By this time the party numbered thirteen—the two climbers, four Kurds and seven Cossacks. They left at 1 am the following morning and began to ascend from the meadows towards a number of parallel ridges which ran up towards the summit in a west-north-westerly direction

After about half an hour they came to the first steep part of the mountain and here both Cossacks and Kurds threw themselves down on the ground for the first of a series of obligatory rests which became ever more frequent, until a monotonous pattern of ten minutes climbing with eight minutes rest was established. 'It was quite useless to expostulate with them, let alone lose one's temper, as they were all in high good humour.'

When the sun finally illuminated the upper part of the mountain, just before 6 am, they were still some 1,830m below the summit and final demoralisation now set in when one of the Kurds had the misfortune to discover a small spring, actually a trickle from a patch of snow, and there the Cossacks played havoc with the flask of Scotch whisky which Mackay had been incautious enough to produce. By the time Bryce called a halt to eat breakfast, the party was reduced to two Cossacks and four Kurds.

It was at this point, about 3,650m up, that Bryce decided to go for the summit alone—how one sympathises with him!

It was an odd position to be in: guides of two different races, unable to communicate either with us or with one another, guides who could not lead and would not follow, guides one-half of whom were supposed to be there to save us from being robbed and murdered by the other half, but all of whom, I am bound to say, looked for the moment equally simple and friendly, the swarthy Iranian as well as the blue-eyed Slav.

At eight o'clock he set off, taking with him some stale bread, a lemon, four hard-boiled eggs, cold tea, meat lozenges and his ice-axe. Much to his surprise the two Cossacks and one of the Kurds fell in behind him.

Almost immediately they came to snow lying on loose scree, but quite soon the going became easier and by 10 am Bryce was looking down on the flat top of Little Ararat where there was no sign of any volcanic crater. At a height of over 3,900m he found his piece of wood—it was about 4ft long and 5in thick, evidently cut by some tool, and so far above the treeline that it could not possibly be a natural fragment. Pouncing on it with a glee that astonished the Cossack and the Kurd (the other had already gone off),

I held it up to them, made them look at it, and repeated several times the word 'Noah'. The Cossack grinned, but he was such a cheery, genial fellow that I think he would have grinned whatever I had said. ... Whether it was really gopher wood, of which material the Ark was built, I will not undertake to say, but I am willing to submit to the inspection of the curious the bit which I cut off with my ice-axe and brought away. ... I am, however, bound to admit that another explanation of the presence of this piece of timber on the rocks at this vast height did occur to me.

Now Bryce began to traverse a snow-slope, cutting steps as he went, assisted by the remaining Cossack who, armed with Mackay's ice-axe, had rapidly assimilated the technique. It was at about this time that the last Kurd turned back. At 10.30 am, at a height of around 4,150m, the Cossack indicated that he would go no further and certainly Bryce could hardly blame him, having noted the condition of his boots, with which the lava rock had played hell.

'I am no disciple of that doctrine of mountaineering without guides which some English climbers have of late preached zealously by example as well as precept, and which others, among them so high an authority as my friend Mr. Leslie Stephen, have wisely set themselves to discourage,' Bryce wrote at this point in his narrative. 'But if there is any justification for the practice, that justification exists when guides are not to be had.'

The next part consisted of a straightforward but extremely exhausting stretch of scree set at an angle of 33 degrees, by Bryce's calculation, in which the stones, basalt, trachyte basalt, amygdaloid, 'and so forth', tended to roll downhill by their own accord, producing a surface on which for every few steps forward 'I slipped down nearly as much as I went up'.

He was also, as he constantly admits, extremely unfit, having taken no exercise whatever, except to be jolted in a tarantass (Russian 4-wheeled, unsprung carriage), since leaving Britain, and at this high altitude he found himself suffering from fatigue and breathlessness which forced him to halt every couple of steps or so to gasp for breath. It was now about 12.30 pm and Bryce sat down near the top of what he described as 'this repulsive stone slope', to eat a hard-boiled egg and further consider his position, something which every mountaineer has done at some time or other. While doing so he came to the conclusion that in order to reach the bivouac where he had left Mackay by 6 pm, which was absolutely necessary in order to avoid being benighted on the upper parts of

Douglas William Freshfield, one of the great mountain explorers, is particularly noted for his expeditions to the Caucasus. His visit in 1868 was the first exploration by a foreigner of the region. In the course of it he climbed Kazbek (16,546ft) but his attempt on Ararat was unsuccessful (*RGS*)

the mountain, he would have to turn back when either 'a bad place' presented itself, or three o'clock arrived. . . . In coming to this decision, there was a sense of relief; and both lungs and legs were so exhausted that the bad place, or three o'clock, would have been almost welcome. Above him now was a line of black cliff from which depended icicles, 60m long, and to escape from the treadmill of the scree Bryce moved off to the left onto a rock rib,

> composed of toppling crags of lava, along whose farther or western side . . . it was possible to work one's laborious way over the fallen masses. Here, a grand sight, perhaps the grandest on the whole moun-tain, presented itself. At my foot was a deep, narrow, impassable gulley, a sort of gigantic *couloir*, in whose bottom snow lay where the inclination was not too steep. Beyond it a line of rock towers, red, grim and terrible, ran right up towards the summit,

its upper end lost in the clouds, through which, as at intervals, they broke or shifted, one could descry, far, far above, a wilder-ness of snow.

From this impossible position Bryce re-treated until he was able to descend into the snow basin. From here he climbed up a bare slope of extremely rotten rocks which he estimated to be at angles of between 38 and 43 degrees. They gave off a loathsome smell. Here, too, the ground exuded 'patches of whitish and reddish yellow stuff', both caused, according to Abich, by 'the natural decomposition of the trachytic rock, which is full of minute crystals of iron pyrites. This, in disintegrating under the moisture of these heights, gives off sulphuric acid gas'.

Whether he knew about these origins before or after the climb, Bryce had other things on his mind at the time, crawling up this interminable rock slope towards what seemed to be a snow-field of which all but the lower part was shrouded in thick mist.

From this tremendous height Little Ararat looked more like a broken obelisk than an independent summit 3,900m in height. Clouds covered the farther side of the great snow basin, and were seething like waves about the savage pinnacles. . . . With mists to the left and above, and a range of black precipices to the right, there came a vehement sense of isolation and solitude, and I began to understand better the awe with which the mountain silence inspires the Kurdish shepherds. Overhead the sky had turned from dark blue to an intense bright green, a colour whose strangeness seemed to add to the weird terror of the scene.

It was now 2 pm and only an hour remained before he would have to put into practice his resolution to turn back; but then, quite suddenly, he found himself on almost level snow and enveloped in a screaming west wind which, at this altitude, enveloped the lower part of his face in ice. He walked on, into the dense cloud, trailing his ice-axe on the snow behind him to mark his return route until suddenly, after five or six minutes, with that dramatic effect which distinguishes so many great ascents, 'the ground began to fall away to the north; I stopped, a puff of wind drove off the mists on one side, the opposite side to that by which I had come, and showed the Araxes plain at an abysmal depth below. It was the top of Ararat.'

In spite of the mountain having been climbed many times, as well as having been thoroughly surveyed, the belief that the Ark was still somewhere on its slopes persisted into the twentieth century. In the 1940s, US flyers reported what appeared to them to be some sort of vessel at a height of about 14,000ft. However, no trace of it was found and as one Frenchman wrote comparatively recently, with the infuriating logic of his race '*Aucun fait n'est venu confirmer l'existence du vaisseau anté-diluvien*'. (Not one fact has appeared to confirm the existence of the antediluvian vessel.)

The Wetterhorn and the landscape round Grindelwald (*F. Villiger-Zefa*)

The Canadian Rockies, Mount Robson (*E. Streichan-Zefa*)

Mount Ararat (*Turkish Tourism Information Office*)

NEW ZEALAND

11 Mount Cook

In 1882 the first of a number of determined attempts was made to reach the summit of New Zealand's highest mountain, Mount Cook (12,349ft). Twelve years were to elapse before anyone succeeded.

Mount Cook (the Maori name for it is *Aorangi*, the cloud-piercer) is in the central section of the Southern Alps which, together with the great Fiordland Plateau, forms the backbone of the South Island.

The peaks of the Southern Alps are lower than those of their European counterparts. Seventeen exceed 10,000ft, a number which up to now, has had to be frequently revised and increased as a result of fresh surveys, and 223 reach around 7,500ft.

In the Southern Alps, more or less in the same latitude south as the European Alps in the north, the snow-line is about 2,000ft lower, at between 6 and 7,000ft, and the glaciers have a higher rate of flow, extending down to a lower altitude.

The Southern Alps provide tough and dangerous climbing. There are far fewer tourist routes to summits than in Europe and the climbing is mostly over snow and ice. The rock is schist and something called 'grey-wacke', a conglomerate of pebbles and sand. The weather can be vile, mid-January to the end of March is the best time; avalanches are common. Even the so-called easiest route to the summit of Mount Cook, by way of the Linda Glacier, can be dangerous because of frequent avalanches and its South-East Face above the Caroline Glacier is the most dangerous of all—Hillary practised on Mount Cook before Everest.

In 1882 the Reverend William Spotswood Green, a thirty-five year old Church of Ireland clergyman made his gallant attempt on Mount Cook, together with Emil Boss and Ulrich Kaufmann of Grindelwald where Boss, a first class climber, was a member of the family who owned the Gasthof Bär.

They made their attack up the great Tasman Glacier from a first camp below it at a height of about 2,300ft. Altogether they set up four camps on the glacier itself, the highest being at about 3,750ft at its junction with the Ball Glacier and the distance between Camps 1 and 5 was only about 9 miles as the crow flies.

The reason for this close spacing was that between them the three men had to carry a total load of 233lb, 129lb of which was equipment, including a gun and cartridges, 104lb being food and fuel—25lb of this was duck and half-boiled mutton taken off the bone to save weight. Of this total Green carried 35lb, which was the most, as he wrote, that he could attempt to carry, while Boss and Kaufmann between them humped an awe-inspiring 198lb, of which Kaufmann took about 112lbs—this in day temperatures on the glacier which rose to well over 90°F in the shade.

On 25 February they made an unsuccessful attempt to reach the South Ridge of Mount Cook by way of the Ball Glacier; but with the summit looming 5,000ft above them they were forced to turn back at a height of 7,500ft on an unstable snow ridge which overlooked the Hooker Glacier to the west.

Immediately on our right the saddle contracted to a narrow snow arête [Green wrote] with a cornice curling over towards the slopes by which we had ascended, and

Mount Cook: the three peaks are on the left, Mount Tasman on the right. Green's route is hidden by the black ridge that drops from the right of the highest (right-hand) peak. The plateau of the Linda Glacier extends right from the bottom of the ridge with the Hochstetter icefall below it. The Tasman Glacier is at the foot of the picture (*John Pascoe*)

ended against a tower of splintered slates some forty feet high. Cautiously advancing along the thin edge of snow we reached these rocks, and found them so loose that we could obtain no hand-grips which would bear the least pressure. Boss and I secured ourselves while Kaufmann climbed round the base of the first crag on hands and knees, and when he was safe we followed. We found ourselves on a ridge connecting the first crag with the second which was about twenty feet higher, and so loose, that I believe we could have shoved it over in either direction, had we had any firm ground to rest on; but the tottering ridge on which we stood trembled beneath our feet, as if undecided whether to tumble towards a big crevasse in the steep glacier to our right, or go thundering down into the Hooker Valley.

On 27 February from their fifth camp they made an attempt to reach what Green called the East Spur of the mountain, by way of a couloir on the north side of the Ball Glacier. In this way they hoped to get above the great ice-fall of the Hochstetter Glacier which pours down onto the Tasman Glacier from the upper ice-fields between Mount Tasman and Mount Cook.

The Ball Glacier was the first obstacle. It stood up in great vertical slabs of ice with perfectly perpendicular walls separated from one another by narrow deep crevasses running parallel with the general course of the glacier. Selecting a narrow edge of ice we cut steps up it, and after traversing the smooth faces of some big ice-blocks, in which we had not only to cut steps for our feet but also little pits for hand grips, we gained the upper surface of the glacier and found by the aneroid that we were already 200ft above our camp.

By noon they had reached a point 3,000ft above the Tasman Glacier at the foot of a series of impossible cliffs which separated

The following five drawings illustrate moments of Green's so nearly successful assault on Mount Cook

The three men attempt the eastern spur

The Reverend William Spotswood Green, 35 year-old Church of Ireland clergyman, who made a gallant attempt on the summit with his two guides, Emil Boss and Ulrich Kaufmann of Grindelwald where Boss's family owned the Gasthof Bär (*Mansell Collection*)

them from the lip of the upper glacier; and from where they were, they could see the plateau of the Hochstetter Glacier above the ice-fall to their right.

From this disagreeable place, where an enormous rock avalanche roared down a couloir close by them, they managed to gain the foot of the couloir which they had set out to climb; but when they reached the top of it they found that they were separated from the glacier plateau by an enormous abyss and from this point, after a further dangerous climb, unroped, up some very steep, yellow sandstone crags they found themselves at about 8,000ft on what Kaufmann called a 'horn'. It was unclimbable and, with precipices on either side, it was impossible to traverse from it.

Their next attempt was made on 1 March by way of what Green called the Mount Tasman Spur, the ridge on the far, northern side of the Hochstetter Glacier. They took with them their usual equipment for such attacks: an oil cloth sheet, an opossum rug, one sleeping bag, provisions for three days, two 60ft ropes, ice-axes and photographic apparatus.

Soon they were forced to climb the face of the Spur on which

> every cleft [Green wrote] was adorned with the edelweiss in full bloom, and every spot to which herbage could cling bore its tufts of snow grass and quantities of little *euphrasia* almost identical, to a casual observer, with the eyebright of our northern land. . . . Many plants which we had found on the other spurs were absent. . . . as might have been expected, because the ridge we were now on was completely isolated, and no seed could arrive on its slopes except through the air.

The day was warm and they suffered from thirst.

By 5 pm they had reached a point below the Hochstetter Dome (8,000ft). To the northwest the Dome looks out over the ice-field

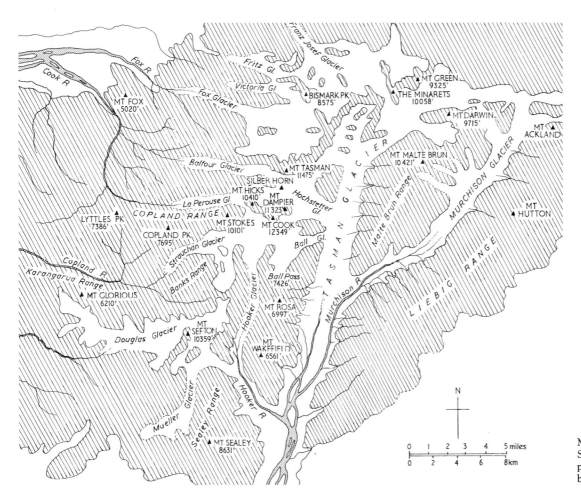

Mount Cook and part of the Southern Alps (Based on a map published in the *Alpine Journal* by kind permission)

called the Great Plateau below Mount Tasman and the Silberhorn, and to the west over the Linda and Adamson Glaciers. All three of these glaciers feed the Hochstetter. Here they bivouacked for the night.

While Kaufmann scraped a smooth place under the rock, arranging stones with their sharpest angles downwards and making a nice bed for us of material somewhat like road metal, Boss and I melted snow by spreading it out thinly on boulders which still retained some of the sun's heat. By due observance of the laws of hydrostatics and capillary attraction, we guided the drops into my drinking cup and the little saucepan of the spirit lamp, and when enough was melted we boiled a cup of

Liebig [a forerunner of Bovril] for supper.

At 6 am the following morning they moved on. 'Great banks of cloud had settled in the valley: out of which the mountain peaks rose like islands, clear cut against one of those pea-green skies so peculiar to New Zealand. Other fleecy masses had sailed aloft to the summits of the higher range. . . .'

A short climb took them to the Hochstetter Dome where the rising sun was on the point of illuminating the upper glaciers.

From the Dome they made the crossing of the Great Plateau to the Linda Glacier, wearing blue-tinted goggles, for by now the sun was shining on the snow and ice from a cloudless sky.

Some of the snow-bridges were so fragile

97

Among the seracs above the great plateau

'From the moment we had gained the arête anxiety about beginning the descent filled our minds.'

that they had to be crossed on all fours. 'Many of the crevasses', Green wrote, 'were not bridged at all, so we had to cut down below their brink and, from a firm step, make a stride across the abyss, judiciously paying out rope to each other as the leap was made.'

By 10 am the worst was past and they were on the Linda Glacier close in under the ridge linking Mount Tasman with Mount Cook; but now the weather was beginning to look threatening away to the north and north east, and cloud began to form over the two big peaks, although the hot sun still continued to pour down on the glaciers.

Here, they left the camera and their provisions on a rock (they had already cached the sleeping gear), and began the climb of what they estimated to be the last 3,000ft or so to the summit with Kaufmann leading, doggedly cutting steps in snow with a crust which collapsed as soon as any weight was put on it. Soon, however, they were on ice so hard that the adze failed to cut it, and even the spike had to be used below the ridge at the head of the Linda Glacier, of which nothing could be seen because of the mist driving over it from the north west.

They were ascending a couloir nearly parallel with the North Ridge, and 'when a report from above the mist told us that an avalanche was coming, we clung onto the crags as the ice-blocks splintered themselves on the sides of the gulley. Some of the blocks whizzed over our heads with a scream like a shot from a 35-ton gun'.

At the upper end of the couloir, where they

had abandoned it for the neighbouring rocks, they found themselves at the source of the avalanche, a great and impassable ice-cliff composed of loose *séracs*.

It was now after 3 pm and the problem was whether to go on or give up. ' "We will top the peak if we go on", said Boss, "To turn now is to give it up altogether". The 24,000 miles of travelling also rose in our minds as a strong argument against retreat.' By 4 pm they were at about 11,000ft; but by now the weather was extremely threatening. However, a temporary clearing of the sky above them showed them the slope rounding off to the summit and the last rock on the North Ridge a short distance above them to their left.

Green now asked Kaufmann how long he thought it would take to climb the slope.

'He said an hour at least. They asked me was I ready to spend a night on the peak? I said I was; so at it we went, Kaufmann sending the ice flying at every blow of his axe.'

By now a thaw had set in, showers of disintegrated ice poured down on them and soon their limbs were soaked. Nevertheless, by 5.30 pm they had succeeded in reaching a *bergschrund* which formed a moat around the edge of the peak.

At 6 pm, after turning this *bergschrund* by a cornice they reached the North Ridge of Mount Cook, and advanced along it, through swirling, inky-black clouds towards the summit.

From the moment we had gained the arête [Green wrote] anxiety about begin-

ning the descent had filled our minds—as should darkness overtake us on the summit of the mountain, our chances of ever returning to the haunts of men would be but slight ... if it came on to blow any harder we would not be able to hold our grip. There was no chance of a view. We were hundreds of feet above any rocks, so that we could build no cairn or leave any record of our ascent. We were all agreed that we were fairly on the summit of the peak, and that we ought to commence the descent.

The decision to go back was made for them when they encountered another *bergschrund* in the cornice on the ridge which would take, Kaufmann estimated, at least twenty precious minutes to turn, out of about sixty minutes of daylight which remained to them. And at this point, 12,317ft by Green's aneroid, actually about 12,150ft some 200ft below the summit, they turned back.

The descent exceeded their worst expectations. Night fell and there were torrents of freezing rain; they spent the night standing on a ledge 2ft wide and over 10,000ft up, sucking Brand's meat lozenges and telling stories and singing songs to keep awake. At 4.30 the next morning (3 March) the sun came up and by 8.30 they found the knapsack of provisions they had left on the Linda Glacier and were soon 'discussing some cold duck and bread'.

After this gallant climb, so little short of complete success, no less than five attempts

were made between 1886 and 1890 by Arthur P. Harper, founder of the New Zealand Alpine Club and a noted surveyor/explorer, and George Edward Mannering; but they too just failed at about 140ft from the summit.

The mountain was finally conquered on Christmas Day, 1894, by a party of three New Zealanders, George Graham, Jack Clarke and their leader Thomas C. Fyfe, one of the pioneer guides of the Southern Alps. Fyfe also made the dramatically difficult traverse of Mount Cook, together with Peter Graham, another famous professional guide, Samuel Turner, a climber from Manchester, and another called Ross. Fyfe and his party were inspired to make their climb by the news that the wealthy amateur, Edward FitzGerald, together with the well-known guide, Matthias Zurbriggen of Macugnaga, had sailed from Europe with the intention of climbing Mount Cook—indeed they arrived in New Zealand only a week before the three New Zealanders reached the summit.

So near and yet so far. Green and his guides were forced to turn back, only some 200ft from the summit

The perilous night on the 2ft ledge over 10,000ft up

FitzGerald had just finished accompanying Martin Conway on part of his great traverse of the Alps, from Monte Viso to the Gross Glockner, which he made with two Gurkhas, and of which he wrote a famous account in *The Alps from End to End* (1895).

FitzGerald was bitterly disappointed at being forestalled and in fact made only the slightest references to Fyfe's climb in his book, *Climbs in the New Zealand Alps*. Nevertheless, in spite of renouncing the climb, together with Zurbriggen, he made a number of important first ascents, including Mount Tasman (11,475ft), Mount Sefton (10,359ft), Mount Haidinger (10,059ft), Silberhorn (10,756ft) and Mount Sealy (8,631ft). For these climbs they used a Mummery tent made of mackintosh sheeting with a sewn-in groundsheet of the same material. Of the four by far the most difficult was Mount Sefton. It was there, while climbing a 300ft perpendicular cliff, with Zurbriggen leading, that a boulder fell on FitzGerald knocking him clean off the face and causing him to describe a complete somersault in mid-air before he was brought up by the rope. It was by some miracle that he did not drop the ice-axe on which their lives depended.

Edward FitzGerald was forestalled in his attempt on Mount Cook by three New Zealanders, George Graham, Jack Clarke and their leader Thomas C. Fyfe, pioneer guide of the Southern Alps. They reached the top on Christmas Day 1894. FitzGerald, however, made a number of successful first ascents including Mount Tasman and Mount Sefton, by far the most difficult. The illustration shows how his guide, Zurbriggen, saved him when a falling boulder knocked him off the face (*Alpine Club*)

THE AMERICAN
CONTINENTS

12 Aconcagua

In the eighteenth century the French geographer, mathematician and physicist, Charles Marie de la Condamine, led a scientific expedition that established the height of the extinct volcano, Chimborazo (20,577ft), the highest peak in the Ecuadorian Andes and the highest mountain then known in the world. The great German scientist and indefatigable explorer, Alexander von Humboldt, attempted to climb it in 1802 and got to 19,286ft, the greatest height known to have been reached by man at that time. Cold and nausea compelled his party to turn back.

In 1883, Aconcagua, a 22,835ft peak in the Central Andes, the highest in the Western Hemisphere, was attempted by Professor Paul Güssfeldt of Berlin University, one of the great climbers of the day. It is a mountain which fearful gales, bitter cold, unstable rocks and the rarefied atmosphere combine to make repellent, and one to which, at that time, no route was known from the outside world. With no companions other than three Chilian *huasos* (drivers) Güssfeldt approached it from the north and set up his modest camp—he had no tent—at 11,750ft in a valley which he named the Penitente, where there was just enough greenery to keep his mules alive. The only other human being, a skeleton clad in rags, he saw while on his way, the following day, to climb the great 3,000ft rock wall which confronted him, which he named the Sierra delle Penitente. On it he reached a gap in the ridge, the Büssertor (16,500ft), and was able to look out over a snow-field to the black, northern slopes of Aconcagua. That day, with support, he might have reached the summit.

The next day, 20 February, after leaving his base at 4 pm, with two of the *huasos*, he reached the Büssertor at 10.30 pm and continued to climb throughout the night, by the light of the moon, crossing the snow-field. At 10 am one of his men collapsed with frozen feet on the slopes, but Güssfeldt and the other *huaso* continued for another six hours, until about 4 pm, by which time they were at about 21,500ft, only about 1,300ft below the summit. Now the sky grew dark and sleet began to fall and Güssfeldt with no resources to fall back on, was forced to retreat. That night he and his *huasos* were back at their tentless bivouac in the valley after more than thirty hours on the mountain without sleep and with scarcely any food.

A second attempt on 4 March, made with two of the *huasos*, was less successful, because Güssfeldt was suffering from an abscess of the gums which was so agonising that he had to treat it with a massive dose of opium. The night was spent at the foot of the mountain on the far side of the ice-field—all three men sharing one sleeping bag in rare discomfort—but the following morning heavy snow forced them to give up short of his previous highest point. No more brave and well conducted attempt on an unknown mountain by a lone mountaineer has ever been made. The comparisons between the extremely modest Güssfeldt's expedition and that of the costly ponderous, ill conceived but victorious expedition of FitzGerald, made fourteen year later, are instructive. Güssfeldt's North Face route was not finally completed until 1951 by another Austro-German expedition.

Aconcagua was finally climbed on 14 January 1897 from the west side, by way of

The extinct volcano, Chimborazo (20,563ft), the highest peak in the Ecuadorian Andes. When its height was established by the French geographer and mathematician, Charles Marie de la Condamine in the eighteenth century, it was the highest mountain then known in the world (*RGS*)

the Horcones Glacier. The successful expedition was led by Edward FitzGerald who had with him Matthias Zurbriggen of Macugnaga who had been with him in the New Zealand Alps in 1895. Besides the other climbing members they had five Swiss and Italian porters.

It was ostensibly a well found and well organised expedition. For the high camps special silk-covered eiderdown sleeping bags were provided which weighed less than 4lb but were totally inadequate at 14,000ft and above. Likewise, the eulogies which Fitz-Gerald bestowed on the rations provided make one feel, having read his account of the expedition, that they must have been written before he set off. He certainly took great pains in his preparations. Before leaving Europe he set up a trial camp at 13,000ft on the Hohberg Glacier near Zermatt, the highest point at which he was able to do so because of bad weather; but this did little to prepare the climbers for the rarefied atmosphere on Aconcagua.

Two days before Christmas they suc-

ceeded in setting up a camp at the snout of the Horcones Glacier (14,000ft). By this time a number of the party were already suffering from mountain sickness and were not helped by the indigestible rations. At their next camp at 16,000ft, which was intensely cold, their cooker refused to work.

On Christmas morning. . . . As we were unable to cook anything, we were obliged to fall back on some tins of Irish stew, melting the great white frozen lumps of grease slowly in our mouths, and then swallowing them. The natural result of this was violent fits of nausea. I now saw the hopelessness of any serious attempt being made till a suitable provision of wood was brought up, with which we could make fires, and cook our food [FitzGerald wrote]. What one requires at these altitudes is light nourishment such as is given to invalids recovering from severe fever.

That afternoon, feeling weak about the knees and having to halt frequently to breathe,

Edward FitzGerald made an attempt on Aconcagua. He had with him Matthias Zurbriggen, a famous guide who made the first ascent, alone, in 1897. He accompanied FitzGerald in the New Zealand Alps in 1895. This picture was taken at their camp below Mount Cook. Zurbriggen is standing and FitzGerald sits on a chair. On Aconcagua their extensive equipment included silk-covered sleeping bags (*Alexander Turnbull Library, Wellington*)

FitzGerald and Zurbriggen reached a height of 19,000ft from which they could see, some 3,500ft above them, a point only 150ft below the summit. It then began to blow a gale from the north west and at the same time FitzGerald was attacked with such violent nausea that they were forced to go down.

Another hideously cold night was passed at 16,000ft, during which the only warm sustenance they had was coffee, heated with spirits of wine which had been brought up from the valley. Some of the men were so cold that they cried like children.

The next day, 26 December, their highest camp was set up at about 18,700ft and meanwhile Zurbriggen reached a height which he estimated to be about 20,700ft, from which point, he reported, the peak looked as far away as it had the previous day. On the descent, utterly exhausted after a whole day on the mountain, he discovered Güssfeldt's visiting card in a tin box which the German climber had buried under a heap of stones, and on the 27th, with the mercury showing 25 degrees of frost, FitzGerald ordered a retreat to the camp at 12,000ft in the Horcones Valley where the morning temperature inside their tents the following day was 90°F. As soon as they reached the valley their symptoms of mountain sickness disappeared.

On 30 December, this time with more blankets, fresh food and fuel, they returned to the 17,000ft camp and the following day, with the mercury registering only 6°F, they again set off for the summit.

At about 20,000ft Zurbriggen's feet became so badly frostbitten that he narrowly escaped losing them. It was with the greatest difficulty that they got him back to camp.

After two further abortive attempts from their 17,000ft camp, having suffered from nausea, headaches and extreme cold, another effort was made on 14 January. The principal obstacle was above 20,000ft, a steep slope covered with loose stones 'that kept rolling, rolling as if to engulf us'.

By this time most of the party seemed in better condition. It consisted of FitzGerald,

The North-West and West Faces of Aconcagua. Bottom left is the Horcones Glacier in the valley where FitzGerald's camp was set up. The ascent was made on the West side of the North Face (*Swiss Foundation for Alpine Research*)

View from West Face of
Aconcagua. The smaller peak on
the right is Cerro Cuerno (*Swiss
Foundation for Alpine Research*)

(*Far right*) Miss Annie S. Peck,
who must have been one of the
few women of her time to
climb in the Andes. She made
the first ascent of the North
Peak of Huascaran (21,834ft)
in the Peruvian Andes in 1908
(*Brown Brothers*)

Zurbriggen and two of the porters, Nicola Lanti and Louis Pollinger. They left their 18,700ft camp at 7 am and by about 9.30, deliberately climbing very slowly to conserve their strength on the terrible stones, they had reached Güssfeldt's cairn. From this point Pollinger was sent off to climb to the west side of the North Ridge where they had left a knapsack containing a bottle of champagne at nearly 22,000ft on one of their previous attempts, while the rest of the party followed the easier, eastern side which was sheltered from the wind which had now risen once more. At 12.30 they reached a point about a thousand feet below the main, east peak where Pollinger eventually met them.

Unbelievable though it seems, at this great height, around 21,800ft, they somehow managed to light a fire with wood brought up from below, and after half an hour succeeded in producing some warm soup. Unfortunately the champagne bottle burst because of the altitude '. . . though we might have known that this would happen, yet so much importance can trifles assume—it discouraged us greatly', FitzGerald wrote.

As a result of this halt for food FitzGerald once more began to suffer from mountain sickness and was unable to continue.

Of my disappointment I need not write, but the object of my expedition was to conquer Aconcagua; I therefore sent Zurbriggen on to complete the ascent. . . . Three-quarters of an hour after he had left, I saw him four hundred feet above me, going across the face of the big stone slope on the way to the saddle between the two peaks. Then for the first time the bitter feeling came over me that I was being left behind, just beneath the summit of the great mountain I had so long been thinking about, talking about, and working for. . . . I got up, and tried once more to go, but I was only able to advance from two to three steps at a time, and then I had to stop, panting for breath, my struggles alternating with violent fits of nausea. . . .

Pollinger had already been sent down to the high camp and it was the Italian, Lanti, who was also fit enough to have reached the summit, in FitzGerald's view, who now accompanied him on his desperately slow descent.

Meanwhile Zurbriggen had reached the summit at 4.45 pm, his only real difficulty during the climb being in breathing. There he erected a 'stone man', a cairn 6½ft high to which he fixed FitzGerald's ice-axe. After spending an hour on the summit, a square plateau about 225ft across, he began the descent and reached the 18,700ft camp three and a half hours later, greatly fatigued, where the party endured another hideous night.

The ascent of the South Face of Aconcagua, considered to be one of the greatest mountaineering feats carried out in the Andes, was performed by a party led by the French climber, R. Ferlet, in 1951.

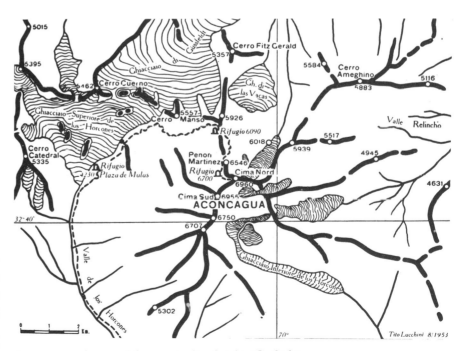

Aconcagua and some of the surrounding heights (*LeAnde*)

13 Mount McKinley

In 1897, after a number of attempts which began eleven years previously, an Italian expedition, led by the Duke of Abruzzi, finally succeeded in climbing Mount St Elias (18,008ft) in the mountains of that name in south-east Alaska—a fifty-seven day, combined operation which involved landing on a surf-swept shore, and the crossing of a series of extremely difficult glaciers, as well as being almost eaten alive by mosquitoes.

If Mount St Elias was difficult Mount McKinley (20,320ft) in Central Alaska, the highest mountain in North America, proved to be even more so.

The people on the east side of the mountain called it Traleika, those who hunted caribou up to the north-western foot of it called it Denali—both Indian names mean the 'Great One'—and it was not until 1896 that it got its more mundane appellation.

In that year gold was discovered in the Yukon, and William McKinley successfully ran for President of the United States. The mountain was named after him by William A. Dickey, a Princeton graduate who had become a gold prospector. Dickey made a shrewd guess at its height, which he put at 23,000ft. He chose the name because the President was a supporter of the gold standard.

Mount St Elias showing the route followed by the Duke of the Abruzzi on the first ascent in 1897. They climbed up the Newton Glacier to Russell Col and thence left to the summit.

The Massif, of which the South Peak of Mount McKinley is the crown, forms the central part of the Alaska Range, extending for a distance of 150 miles from Rainy Pass at its south-western end to the valley of the Nenana river in the north-east, through which the railway runs from Anchorage, on the Pacific coast, to Fairbanks, 356 miles away in the interior.

There are twenty-one peaks in the McKinley Massif, all of more than 10,000ft. Of these two exceed 13,000, one 14,000, one 17,000 and two 19,000ft. The North Peak of Mount McKinley is 19,470ft and the great South Peak 850ft higher. The massif also contains within it some of the world's largest glaciers—three more than 30 miles, and two more than 40 miles long; the longest is the 46-mile Kahiltna Glacier below the south-west face of the South Peak. On almost every count Mount McKinley poses great problems to mountaineers, some of them unique.

To this day it is still extremely remote. The nearest road (until the Denali Highway was built) was 29 miles to the north, while the nearest railway is 45 miles south, both as the crow flies. Because it is in the Mount McKinley National Park, aircraft, unless working in conjunction with scientific or government-sponsored bodies, are not allowed to land near it. Even air-drops of supplies are strictly controlled. It has, too, the greatest base-to-summit rise of any mountain on earth—17,000ft above the plateau on which it stands. Everest only rises 13,000ft above the monastery at the Rongbuk Glacier.

'The shortest possible route to the top of Mount McKinley requires no less than 36 miles of walking, one way, not taking into account relaying of zigzagging, in addition to 18,500ft of vertical climbing.' So wrote Bradford Washburn, the great American climber. He himself climbed the mountain three times—what was the third ascent of it, in 1942, again in 1947 with his wife and a third time, in 1951, by way of the West Buttress. Another of Washburn's great achievements was the conquest of Mount Lucania (17,150ft), Canada's second highest mountain, in the Yukon section of the Mount St Elias Mountains.

Thirty-five degrees and 2,400 miles further north than Everest—only 3½ degrees south of the Arctic Circle—the climate of Mount McKinley is sub-Arctic. It has the world's greatest rise above the tree-line and, with a snow-line at 4,000ft, one of the greatest extents of vertical snow cover.

And it is cold. In May and June temperatures can fall to 30°F, or more, below zero and winds in the same months often attain velocities of a hundred or more miles an hour. In winter the temperatures on the summit drop to 50 and 60 degrees below zero. The mountain also lies in an extremely active earthquake zone.

The obstacles surrounding the mountain were well summed up by the mysterious and elusive Dr Frederick A. Cook, who made two attempts at it, in 1903 and 1906. In the June 1904 *Bulletin* of the American Geographical Society he wrote:

The area of this mountain is far inland, in the heart of a most difficult and trackless country, making the transportation of men and supplies a very arduous task. The thick underbush, the endless marshes, and the myriads of vicious mosquitos bring to the traveller the troubles of the tropics; the necessity of fording and swimming icy streams, the almost perpetual cold rains, the camps in high altitudes on glaciers, in snows and violent storms, bring to the traveller all the discomforts of the arctic explorer; the very difficult slopes, combined with high altitude effects, add the troubles of the worst Alpine climbs. The prospective conquerer of America's culminating peak will be amply rewarded, but he must be prepared to withstand the tortures of the torrids, the discomforts of the North Pole seeker, combined with the hardships of the Matterhorn ascent multiplied many times.

The first attempt to climb it was made by a five-man party under the leadership of Judge James Wickersham in June 1903. They set out from Fairbanks, a boom town since the discovery of gold only 12 miles to the north of it in 1902. They used pack-horses to carry their equipment and made their approach by way of the Peters and Jeffery Glaciers to the foot of the Wickersham Wall (8,000ft), a tremendous ice-face on the north side. Not surprisingly, they turned back here, the Judge convinced that the thing was unclimbable (none of the party had any climbing experience).

That same year a second expedition, led by Dr Cook, made an attempt on the mountain following a route by way of the Peters Glacier, pioneered in 1903 by two surveyors, Brooks and Reaburn. Cook was an experienced explorer. He had been with Robert E. Peary on his expedition to Baffin Bay in 1891, and in 1899 he had been a member of Lieutenant A. de Gerlache's Belgian expedition to the Antarctic; however this expedition also failed

to make much impression, reaching a height of about 11,000ft on the West Buttress of the North Peak.

The next expedition, in 1906, was organised by Cook and Professor Herschel C. Parker, with funds provided by Parker and a wealthy sportsman from the Eastern seaboard who was unable to join the party. Other members were Belmore Browne, a naturalist and artist who wrote an account of this and subsequent expeditions in which he took part (*The Conquest of Mount McKinley*). Altogether the party numbered seven, including two porters, a photographer and a topographer.

From Tyonek, a village on Cook Inlet, which they reached by steamer and a smaller vessel, the party travelled by launch and horse-back north westwards to the upper waters of the Yentna river and then north eastwards across several tributaries of the Yentna on the flanks of the range to reach, eventually, the head of the Tokositna river, the 'river that comes from the land where there are no trees.' They were now on the south-east side of the mountain and from a high point above the Tokositna Glacier they could see the South and West Faces, both of which appeared hopelessly difficult.

When the party returned to Tyonek, Dr Cook announced that he was going to take Ed Barrill, one of the porters and another, newly hired man up the Susitna river which runs due north for some distance from the head of Cook Inlet in the general direction of the mountain. Before leaving he sent a telegram to a New York businessman which read 'Am preparing for a last, desperate attack on Mount McKinley'.

When Cook finally re-appeared at Seldovia, at the south end of Cook Inlet, where Browne was waiting for him, he immediately claimed that he had reached the top from the south. Browne realised that this was impossible in the time Cook had been away—less than a month—and when he asked Barrill what he knew about Mount McKinley he answered, 'I can tell you all about the big peaks just south of the mountain, but if you want to

On the top of Mount St Elias.
The Duke of the Abruzzi is
the right-hand sitting figure
(*Instituto di Fotografa Alpina
'V. Sella'*)

know about Mount McKinley go and ask Cook.'

'I now found myself in an embarrassing position', Browne wrote. 'I knew that Dr Cook had not climbed Mount McKinley. Barrill had told me so and in addition I knew it in the same way that any New Yorker would know that no man could walk from the Brooklyn Bridge to Grant's Tomb in ten minutes.' On his return to civilisation Cook set about publishing his account of his conquest of the mountain, *To the Top of the Continent*. It included a photograph supposed to show Barrill on the summit holding the Stars and Stripes, which was later proved to have been taken on another, far inferior summit, a day's detour up a side glacier, which Browne himself photographed on the next expedition in 1910, while reaching 10,300ft on the south-east flank.

It was not possible to make a formal accusation against Cook until his book was published and by that time he had set off for the Arctic, where he claimed to have reached the North Pole from Axel Heiberg Island on 21 April 1908 in company with two unknown Eskimos, a year before Peary reached it on 5 April 1909. Although he may not have actually reached the Pole, Cook's Arctic journey was, nevertheless, a remarkable one.

The news of Cook's alleged climb was received with equal scepticism by the Sourdoughs (prospectors and trappers) of Fairbanks, and in the winter of 1909 Billie McPhee, a local saloon keeper, offered to finance, to the extent of $500, an attempt on the summit by two local men. He also laid a $5,000 bet that they would reach the summit before 4 July 1910. The result was one of the most heroic amateur exploits in the history of mountaineering.

The protagonists were Tom Lloyd who was nearer sixty than fifty and Billy Taylor and with them went two equally tough trappers, Peter Anderson, a Swede, Charley McGonagall, and two others. They took two dog-sleds, some rope, camping gear and what they hoped would be enough provisions to

Mount McKinley from the north-east looking up the Muldrow Glacier, the route followed by the Sourdoughs to the summit in 1910—one of the most heroic amateur exploits in mountaineering history (*photo by Bradford Washburn, RGS*)

see them through. McPhee's $500 was the extent of their capital. They left on 20 December, in the depths of the winter of 1909, and, by the time they reached the base of the mountain it seems that two unnamed members of the party had already quarrelled with the others and dropped out.

The attack was made by way of what was named the McGonagall Pass to the Muldrow Glacier, a route which the Sourdoughs had chosen, with great acumen, as the most likely way to the summit, and which they reached using dog teams. As high-altitude rations they carried bacon, beans and doughnuts.

Towards the end of March 1910, eleven weeks later, much of the time battered by blizzards, they reached a height of 11,000ft on the glacier and here set up their base camp. The only casualty was Peter Anderson who had one toe frostbitten, but treated it lightly, with the words, 'a little bit sore as a fellow would say'. Then, so the story goes, after waiting some days for the weather to improve, and still using their dog-teams, they

The Sourdoughs, conquerors of the North Summit of Mount McKinley, in their Sunday best; (*left to right*): Charley McGonagall, Peter Anderson, Billy Taylor; Tom Lloyd, seated (*Mount McKinley, the Pioneer Climbs*)

reached a point below the edge of the Karstens Ridge which separates the Muldrow Glacier from the Traleika Glacier to the east. There they set up their final camp in a hole excavated in the ice and, the following day, set off on their final attack on the summit.

At 15,000ft they discovered that there were, in fact, two summits, the North Peak (19,470ft) and the South Peak (20,320ft), about 3¼ miles apart and separated from one another by the width of the Harper Glacier.

It was this photograph, captioned 'The Top of our Continent' which the Sourdoughs (among others) disbelieved. The peak that exposed Cook's fake is just visible in the right-hand top corner (*To the Top of the Continent*)

Unfortunately, they decided to climb the lower North Peak, possibly because, seeing it from certain directions, it is difficult to realise that it is 950ft lower than the South Peak, or possibly because the North Peak was the one from which they hoped their flag-pole would be visible by telescope from Fairbanks when they finally planted it there.

Finally, in early April 1910, wearing home-made crampons and using pole and double-bitted lumber axes, they succeeded in cutting a staircase up the Karstens Ridge, by way of which Anderson and Taylor, carrying a 14ft dry spruce flagpole which they had lugged all the way up from the plain below, reached the North Peak where they set it up with the Stars and Stripes streaming from it.

The descent was accomplished relatively quickly; but, once at Fairbanks, Taylor, who kept a log of the climb, and was the first to return (the others had gone on to work their mining claims), for some reason maintained that the party had climbed both summits—perhaps he was afraid that McPhee

might lose his $5,000 wager which was contingent on the *summit* being reached. In fact, outside Alaska, it was widely disbelieved that either summit had been climbed by the Sourdoughs and it was not until three years later that proof that they had reached the lesser peak was forthcoming.

In 1912, Herschel Parker and Belmore Browne, together with Merl la Voy who had also been on the 1910 expedition, and Arthur M. Aten made another attempt. Following the same route as the Sourdoughs, up the Muldrow Glacier, they set up three high camps at 15,000, 16,000 and 16,615ft and from this last one, where they suffered intensely from cold and an inability to eat pemmican at this altitude, they made two attacks on the summit.

My sleeping-bag weighed seventeen pounds [Browne wrote]. It was large and made of the best blue or 'black' wolf fur. When I was ready to sleep I first enclosed my feet in three pairs of the warmest, dry Scotch-wool socks. In addition I wore two suits of heavy woolen underclothing. Then came heavy woolen trousers covered with canvas 'overalls' which keep the wind from penetrating, and the snow from sticking to the wool trousers. On my upper body I wore two of the heaviest woolen shirts made; they were of grey wool with a double back and large breast pockets that doubled the front thickness. Over these shirts I placed a fine woven Scotch-wool sweater and around my waist I wrapped a long 'muffler' of llama wool. The collars of my shirts were brought close by a large silk scarf, while the ends of wool socks covered my wrists. Over all I wore a canvas 'parka', the universal Alaskan wind shield with a hood trimmed with wolverine fur. My head was covered with a muskrat fur cap which covered my neck and ears and tied under my chin. My hands were protected by heavy Scotch-wool gloves covered with heavy leather gloves, and my feet were enclosed, in addition to the socks,

by heavy soft leather moccasins. ...
Despite the above elaborate precautions I
can honestly say that *I did not have a single
night's normal sleep above 15,000ft on
account of the cold*!

Professor Parker dressed more warmly
than either La Voy or myself. He wore at
night a complete suit of double llama wool
besides his mountain clothing, and yet he
could not sleep for the cold, although
Anthony Fiala, leader of the Ziegler Polar
Expedition slept comfortably in a duplicate
of Professor Parker's bag clad only in
underclothes when the temperature was
70 below zero! This fact illustrates the
comparative effect of cold between sea level
and 15,000ft close to the Arctic circle.

On 29 June, with only 3,500ft to climb,
they left their high camp at 6 am and by mid-
morning, climbing at an estimated rate of
about 400ft an hour, cutting steps as they
went, they had reached 18,500ft more than
the previous altitude record for North
America, established by the Duke of Abruzzi
on Mount St Elias. 'At a little less than
19,000ft we passed the last rock on the ridge',
Browne wrote, 'and secured our first clear
view of the summit. It rose as innocently as
a tilted snow-covered tennis court and as we
looked it over we grinned with relief—we
knew the peak was ours.'

But it was not to be. By the time the three
men reached 19,300ft a blizzard had risen,
at 20,000ft visibility was down to a few feet
and with a wind of more than 50 mph the
cold was so intense, around 15 degrees below
zero, that they could feel it moving up their
limbs from the tips of their toes and fingers.
It was here, on the final dome, only about
200yd and 150 vertical feet from the summit,
with the slope no longer steep, they had to
admit defeat. As Browne said, when Professor
Parker gallantly suggested that they should
continue and that he, too, would cut steps
(Browne and La Voy had so far done this
because they were practised at the work):
'... it was not a question of chopping and

Belmore Browne, Herschel
Parker and Merl la Voy came
within 300ft of the South Peak
in 1912. This is Browne's
drawing of the southern
approach, the one followed by
the Sourdoughs (*Alpine Club*)

La Voy pointed out our backsteps—or the
place where our steps ought to be, for a foot
below us everything was wiped out by the
hissing snow.'

Coming down from the final dome was as
heartless a piece of work as any of us had
ever done. Had I been blind, and I was
nearly so from the trail chopping and
stinging snow, I could not have progressed
more slowly. Every foothold I found with
my axe alone, for there was no sign of a
step left. It took me nearly two hours to
lead down that easy slope of one thousand
feet. ... We reached camp at 7.35 pm after
as cruel and heart-breaking a day as I trust
I will ever experience.

Two days later the weather improved and
they were sufficiently restored to make
another attempt; but again another terrible
blizzard blew up and at 19,300ft they were
forced to turn back. It was cruel luck.

A few days later, by which time they had
reached the base of the mountain, a severe

earthquake occurred. It caused a most spectacular avalanche and also, although of course they did not know this, radically altered the physiognomy of the summit ridge by which they had attacked the mountain.

They had been beaten by the weather; but they had also had dietary problems. Their basic food was supposed to be cooked pemmican, a diet suitable for Arctic conditions but pretty indigestible stuff at high altitudes. Of living conditions at the highest camp (16,615ft), Browne wrote: 'We had now given up all thought of eating pemmican and were living, as in fact we had been living since leaving our 15,000ft camp, on tea, sugar, hardtack (biscuits), and raisins.'

Mount McKinley's South Peak was finally climbed on 7 June 1913, by a four-man team. The leader was the fifty year old Reverend Hudson Stuck, Episcopal Archdeacon of the Yukon, who had already done a lot of climbing in the Rockies. A 'muscular Christian' if ever there was one, he had in fact emigrated from the home of muscular Christianity to North America at the age of twenty-two.

The other members of the party were Harry P. Karstens, a prospector from Fairbanks, Walter Harper, an Alaskan Indian, and Robert Tatum, a young missionary.

Stuck organised his expedition well and naturally followed what had been, before the earthquake, the well pioneered route by way of the Muldrow Glacier. However, the saddle which led to the dome had been altered out of recognition by the earthquake and very much for the worse, and Stuck's party, too, was forced to cut an enormously long staircase up it which they used for bringing up supplies for the final attack on the peak. The first man to the top was Harper who had led throughout the day.

On the way to it they were able to see clearly the 14ft spruce erected as a flag pole by the Sourdough expedition three years before, and it is no denigration of the 1913 climbers, or those who preceded or followed the Sourdoughs on the mountain, to say that theirs was the greatest climb of all.

(*Left*) Professor Herschel C. Parker who, with Dr Frederick A. Cook, organised the 1906 attempt on Mount McKinley. He made another attempt in 1912 when he wore a suit of double llama wool besides his mountain clothing and still could not sleep for the cold (*Brown Brothers*)

Mount Everest. John Evans and a companion in the foreground. He was a member of the International Himalayan Expedition of 1971

Mount Cook, the summit

Mount McKinley

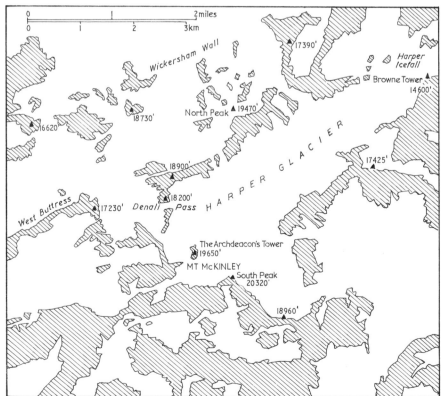

14 The Canadian Rockies

The earliest accurately recorded ascents of the Canadian and other sections of the Rockies, were made by explorers and surveyors. It was James Hector, for example, who went on Captain J. Palliser's expedition of 1857 'to explore the country between the northern branch of the Saskatchewan River and the frontier of the United States, and between the Red River and the Rocky Mountains'—a largish order. He reached Kicking Horse Pass (5,339ft), the watershed between the Pacific and the Atlantic. Thirty years later the pass became the high point on the Canadian Pacific railway line between Montreal and Vancouver, built at a then astronomical cost of $150,000,000, of which between three and four million were consumed by the survey work alone. It was building of the railway, and the subsequent opening up of Lake Louise in the Selkirk Mountains as a tourist area, that made the region more accessible to climbers.

In 1888, two of the three well known English Topham brothers, Harold Ward and Edwin, together with the Reverend William Spotswood Green, who had nearly made the first ascent of Mount Cook six years previously, travelled through the Selkirk Mountains, a 200-mile long range in south-eastern British Columbia, which extends into the great bend of the Columbia river, west of the Rockies. There they made the first ascents of three peaks, Glacier Crest, Terminal Peak and Mount Bonney, the map made from Green's survey of the range being the first ever produced. That same year Harold Topham made his unsuccessful attempt on Mount St Elias, when his party reached 11,375ft on the South Ridge.

Between 1887 and 1897 a number of expeditions were made, purely for the sake of climbing. In 1890, Harold Topham returned to the Selkirks, where he made four first ascents (Mounts Donkin, Fox, Selwyn, Sugar Loaf and Purity)—later Mount Topham was named after him.

The majority of the pioneer climbers in the Canadian Rockies, however, were American and, of these, members of the Appalachian Mountain Club of Boston, founded in 1876 and the first of its kind, were to the fore. The first recorded climbing fatality in North America occurred on Mount Lefroy (11,400ft) on the shore of Lake Louise in August 1896, when one of its members, P. S. Abbot, fell from a wall following a successful attempt on nearby Mount Hector (11,135ft).

Mount Lefroy was climbed the following year by a party which included C. S. Thompson, one of the great pioneers of climbing in the Rockies and the Selkirks, John Norman Collie, a distinguished scientist and the discoverer of neon, and a Swiss guide, Peter Sarbach.

Between 1897 and 1911, Norman Collie who, besides his other mountaineering exploits, was also a great climber of British cliffs, sea and land—he had been on Nanga Parbat with Mummery in 1895—made thirteen first ascents in the Canadian Rockies; some of them, between 1898 and 1902, with three other British climbers, Hermann Woolley, Sydney Spencer and Hugh Stutfield.

In 1898 they discovered the great Columbia Ice-field, the largest in the Canadian Rockies and also interesting because its waters, coming from the slopes of the Snow Dome (11,600ft), flow to the Atlantic, by way of the

Mount Everest. Hillary and Tenzing going up the South Col (*RGS*)

North Saskatchewan river and Hudson Bay; the Pacific, by the Columbia river, and to the Arctic Ocean by way of the Athabasca, the Slave river and the Mackenzie. That year, too, they made four first ascents, all without guides, of the Snow Dome and of Diadem, north of the Ice-field, much the same height and of the Survey Peak (8,500ft), lying west of the big bend where the North Saskatchewan turns eastwards towards the Canadian Plains, and of Mount Thompson (10,700ft). The same year, Woolley made a solo climb of Mount Wilcox, a 10,000ft peak, eastwards of the upper part of the Athabasca. In 1902, they made six more first ascents (Mounts Murchison, Freshfield, Forbes, Noyes and Neptuak, and Howse Peak, all of them south of the Saskatchewan river).

One of the most interesting climbs, because of the natural phenomena they encountered rather than the technical difficulties, was their ascent of Diadem a typically unstable snow-crowned peak, one of three neighbouring summits between the eastern and western branches of the Athabasca river—the other two they named Woolley and Stutfield. From the eastern branch they humped their gear up a canyon to the foot of the Diadem Glacier, but before reaching it were confronted by a remarkable spectacle:

A tremendous rock-fall had evidently taken place from their ugly, bare limestone cliffs; and the whole valley, nearly half a mile wide, was covered to a depth of some hundreds of feet with boulders and *debris* . . .

Stutfield and Collie wrote in their interesting (but on the whole not very exciting) *Climbs and Exploration in the Canadian Rockies*

. . . The immense amount of rock that had fallen on the glacier below Peak Stutfield had prevented the ice from melting. Consequently the glacier, filling up the valley to a depth of at least two hundred feet, had moved bodily down; and its snout, a couple of hundred feet high, covered with blocks of stone the size of small houses, was playing havoc with the pine woods before it and on either side. In our united experiences, extending over the Alps, the Caucasus, the Himalaya, and other mountain ranges, we had never seen indications of a landslide on so colossal a scale.

After bivouacking at the foot of the glacier on beds of heather and pine twigs, they set off the following morning to attack Mount Woolley, but, by the time they reached the foot of the ice-fall leading to the upper part of

The first ascent of Mount Robson in 1913. The party was headed by Albert H. MacCarthy (*centre*). His climbing partner was William W. Foster (*left*) and the great Austrian guide, Conrad Kain (*right*) who had gone to live in British Columbia in 1910. 'Gentlemen, that's as far as I can take you', Kain said when they reached the summit (*Archives of the Canadian Rockies*)

Conrad Kain died in 1934 but the year before he and J. Monroe Thorington made the first ascent of Trapper's Peak (9,790ft). (*Archives of the Canadian Rockies*)

its glacier, a violent downpour of rain caused such a heavy fall of ice from it that they decided to try Diadem instead.

The face, once they had got clear of the scree, was straightforward, some rock chimneys leading to a steep rib which they followed to the summit, but, again, the rock was terribly splintered and insecure.

Standing as we were, near the Great Divide, we looked down on a marvellous complexity of peak and glacier, of low-lying valley, shaggy forest, and shining stream, with here and there a blue lake nestling in the recesses of the hills. Quite close, as it seemed, the overpowering mass of Mount Brown [British Columbia], towered frowning many hundreds of feet above us . . . like a gigantic castle in shape, with terrific black cliffs falling sheer on three sides. A great wall of dark thunder-cloud loomed up over its summit.

They were not given much time to admire the panorama.

All day long there had been a growling of distant thunder in the west, and as we turned to go down the storm burst upon us with a vengeance. It grew very dark; a white driving scud of sleet and hail swept by on the whistling wind, making our ears and faces tingle. The thunder rattled and roared in grand style among the crags; the air was aboil with eddying twisting vapours; and the lightning leaping, as it were, from peak to peak, zig-zagged merrily athwart the sky. More than once we were constrained to stop and take shelter from the drift and sweep of the storm, throwing aside our ice-axes for fear of the lightning, which seemed to be playing all round us. We took the easiest way down the face, taking chances with falling stones. . . . During the night there were more thunderstorms—we had five in twenty-four hours —and the drippings from our leaky tent soaked our already damp sleeping bags;

but we slept soundly through it all.

The first recorded climbing fatality in North America occurred in 1896 on Mount Lefroy (11,400ft) when one of the members of the party Philip Abbott of the Appalachian Club of USA fell from its wall. It was climbed the following year by C. S. Thompson, one of the pioneers of climbing in the Rockies and the Selkirks— the lower figure in the white jersey (*Archives of the Canadian Rockies*)

In 1901 Edward Whymper made the first of three visits to the Rockies—the last one being in 1909. He was accompanied by four Swiss guides, Christian Kaufmann of Grindelwald, Joseph Pollinger, Joseph Bossonay and the great guide Christian Klucker of Sils in the Engadine. He made a number of first ascents; but left no account of them. That same year the Reverend (later Sir) James Outram, another pioneer of Canadian climbing, who had accompanied Whymper on some of his expeditions, succeeded in reaching the top of Mount Assiniboine (11,870ft).

The last big Canadian Rocky Mountain peak to be climbed before World War I was the highest, Mount Robson (12,972ft) in the eastern part of British Columbia near the Alberta border, climbed in the summer of 1913. In appearance, partly because of its isolation, it bears some resemblance to the Matterhorn and, because of the avalanches which rake it, it is a very dangerous mountain.

Mount Edith Cavell (11,033ft) one of the highest peaks in the Rockies (*Douglas Dickins*)

125

It was finally conquered by way of the avalanche-swept north-eastern face by a party headed by the great American-born climber Albert H. MacCarthy, who went to live in British Columbia in 1910. With him were two other members of the climbing partnership which he formed, William W. Foster and the great Austrian guide, Conrad Kain who had first gone to Canada in 1909 at the invitation of the Alpine Club of Canada and subsequently made his home there after visits to Russia and New Zealand. 'Gentlemen,

that's as far as I can take you,' Kain said as he reached the summit after a rather scarey climb which he led the whole way.

In the course of the next three years MacCarthy and Kain made successful attacks on Mount Sir Donald, first climbed by Swiss Alpine Club members Carl Sulzer and Emil Huber in 1900, by way of the North-West Ridge, Mount Louis, a spire which they climbed unroped and, in 1916, together with Mrs MacCarthy, one of the best women climbers of the time in North America, the

Columbia icefield: the snout of the Athabaska Glacier on which tourists travel in snowmobiles. The moraine on the left is 300ft high (*Douglas Dickins*)

Bugaboo Spire, one of the famous granite Bugaboos in the Purcell Range of British Columbia, of which Kain said that the crucial part, up a narrow chimney in a smooth wall without any intermediate belays, was the hardest of his life.

MacCarthy crowned but did not terminate his great career in 1925 (in 1926 he made 101 ascents in the Alps in sixty-three days). In that year he led an expedition which succeeded in climbing Mount Logan in the St Elias Range in the Yukon, the highest peak in Canada and the second highest on the North American continent, a peak extremely difficult to get to—at that time the nearest setting-off point for it was about 140 miles away, the last 70 miles of which had to be covered with dog- or horse-sledges over ice-fields.

The attack began in mid-May 1925, after MacCarthy, his Sourdough guide, Andy Taylor, and three others had spent a large part of the preceding winter setting up supply depots and reconnoitering camp sites.

Mount Logan on the left, King Col and King Peak from the north (*Bradford Washburn*)

It was so cold in February, − 45°F, that the harness of the two horse-drawn sleds froze solid and could not be removed from the animals' backs for a fortnight.'

The party consisted of nine members—there were no porters and each man was called on to hump a 70lb load and haul sledges—and it took them a month to reach King Col from McCarthy in Alaska, where they set up a camp only 6,000ft below the 19,850ft main summit, although still 8 horizontal miles from it.

By June 22, in the teeth of terrible blizzards, in the course of which one member of the party was frostbitten and had to be accompanied off the mountain, they succeeded in setting up a highest camp on the summit plateau at a height of 18,500ft, only 1,350ft below the summit, although still, because of the configuration of this awesome mountain, a long way from it horizontally, which they discovered the following day, 23 June, when they made their final attack.

The Reverend Hudson Stuck, 'a muscular Christian' who was Episcopal Archdeacon of the Yukon, climbed a lot in the Rockies before leading the party that made the first ascent of Mount McKinley in 1913 (*Brown Brothers*)

The party now consisted of MacCarthy, Fred Lambart, the deputy leader, Andy Taylor, Allen Carpé, Norman Read and William Foster.

By 4.30 pm they had reached what they thought to be the summit; but which, in fact, proved to be a subsidiary one. The true summit was between two and three miles away across a concave depression and by the time they had struggled across this gap it was 8 pm.

The descent was a nightmare. Hardly had the six climbers begun it than a fearful storm broke and they were forced to excavate holes in the snow, in which they spent that night and the following day until early afternoon, at a height of 19,000ft in temperatures down to 12 degrees below zero. Even then their descent was rendered extremely difficult by thick cloud and, when they finally picked up a line of willow-wand markers, one rope of three men, MacCarthy's, became disorientated, so for some time they were actually climbing gently towards the summit, while the other three successfully reached the 18,500ft plateau camp. As a result MacCarthy's group, consisting of Carpé and Foster, spent another night in the open and only reached the plateau camp early the following morning.

From there, that same day, the two ropes essayed the vital crossing of the ridge at 18,500ft which would take them down to the King Col and it was at this point, in a raging gale, that Read was sent forward to pathfind the way for the two parties. When he turned to see if they were following, he found that both were leading off in the wrong direction to what would certainly be their deaths. By a miracle he was seen by Carpé and all six men finally reached their lower camp, at around 13,850ft, at one o'clock the following morning. So ended a most gallant but much criticised expedition. The mountain was not climbed again until 1950 when the Swiss climber André Roch and Norman Read, the pathfinder on the first expedition, now a man of sixty, reached the summit.

15 The Yosemite and El Capitan

Some of the toughest rock-climbing anywhere is to be found in the Yosemite Valley, on the western slopes of the Sierra Nevada Range, about 150 miles east of San Francisco. Here, from the mile-deep gorge of the Merced river, facing one another across an abyss between half a mile and a mile wide, loom up some of the most awe-inspiring mural precipices on earth, eroded granite, polished by glacial action, ornamented with spires, domes, gables, battlements and cut into by side canyons: all facing one another on two 7-mile fronts.

One of the men who took up the challenge offered by these great walls was an Easterner, Robert L. M. Underhill, a Harvard mathematician and philosopher, one of the protagonists of climbing in New England as was his wife, Ann Miriam O'Brien. In 1928 he became editor of the journal of the famous Appalachian Club of Boston, the members of which had done so much of the pioneer climbing in the Canadian Rockies back in the 1890s.

It was Underhill's climb, together with Fritiof Fryxell, of the North Face of the Grand Teton, a nearly vertical wall more than 2,000ft high in the Teton Range of Wyoming, previously regarded as unclimbable, that inspired a new generation of American climbers and helped to break down the objections of the old régime to the use of ironmongery, such as pitons and karabiners. In his writings Underhill stressed the fact that these instruments should not be used in a profligate way and that their use demanded a new attitude of mind. In 1931 the Sierra Club invited him to instruct its members in the use of rope on rock and having done so he then went on to climb Mount Whitney (14,495ft) in the High Sierra, the highest mountain in the USA, ouside Alaska. He won the summit by way of the East Face. The other members of the party were Glen Dawson and Jules Eichorn, both students, and Norman Clyde, a famous Sierra Club climber, who used to take volumes of the Greek classics with him, and spent his life climbing in the Sierra. Underhill described this climb, in the Sierra Club *Bulletin* of February 1932, as 'a mere bluff but great fun'. Bluff or not the most difficult face of the highest mountain in the Sierra Nevada had been climbed and this marked the beginning of modern rock-climbing in California.

In the Yosemite Valley the only man who had done any climbing to speak of was the local postmaster, Charles Michael. He was an aquaintance of Eichorn and told him that in his opinion the Cathedral Spires on the south side of Yosemite Valley, opposite El Capitan, were unclimbable.

By this time the Cragmont Climbing Club had been formed and on the rock faces of the Berkeley Hills its members performed important and sometimes Kamikaze-like experiments in the use of pitons and what was called the 'dynamic belay'. Later, in 1933, they became the Rock-Climbing Section of the Sierra Club and, inspired by Eichorn, himself inspired by Michael, some of its members decided to have a shot at the awesome Higher Cathedral Spire and, over the Labour Day holiday of 1933, Eichorn, Dick Leonard and Bestor Robinson embarked on what was an historic first attempt on the 400ft southern flank of the Spire, leaving the North Face—1,000ft sheer—to posterity.

The Yosemite Valley, on the western slopes of the Sierra Nevada Range, some 150 miles from San Francisco, scene of some of the toughest rock-climbing in the world (*John Cleare*)

They had no pitons, only ordinary 10in nails from a hardware store which bent when they stood on them, and the leader's belaying arrangements, with the rope running through a rope sling attached to a nail, sound, even to a novice, like a one-way ticket to eternity. After seven hours they gave up.

Eventually they succeeded in getting enough money together to order some real pitons and karabiners from Munich where pitons had been in production for years since their evolution in 1924 by F. Rigele, for an attack on the North-West Face of the Gross Wiesbachhorn. On their next attempt, with their now-sophisticated equipment and led by Eichorn, they succeeded in traversing the difficult Bathtub Pitch, using rope stirrups, but again failed to reach the top. The following year, in April 1934, they made their third attempt with what in those days sounded like quite a lot of gear. The pitons they had put in on their previous attack were, not surprisingly, still in position and these enabled them to reach their previous highest point,

below a difficult 30ft wall, without much difficulty. On this wall Leonard, a San Francisco Bay law student, led at first with Robinson, an attorney, as his second; but altogether they changed over five times before they succeeded in climbing it. To do so they employed a new system which had already been used in Germany, known as tension climbing, in which the second holds the leader, standing in a stirrup, into the face on one rope, and then, when the leader has hammered in another piton higher up and karabinered his second rope and his stirrup to it, the second man hauls away on the second rope—an efficient system, although exhausting when unduly protracted as it was in this instance.

The greatest obstacle Leonard encountered was an overhang above the 30ft wall. With nothing to get either his fingers or a piton into, he put in a piton below it and got himself lowered about 20ft; then he pendulumed across the face until he found a crack with which he could do nothing, and it was

Eichorn who finally managed to get pitons into it. It proved to be the crucial part of the climb and by sunset they had reached the summit. A few months later they climbed the Lower Spire.

The big climb in 1939 was Shiprock, a volcanic plug full of rotten rock, rising 1,800ft out of the desert in New Mexico, 20 miles south of the Colorado border. It was attempted in 1937 by Robert Ormes, Mel Griffiths, Gordon Williams and Bill House, and in the course of the climb Ormes

had a spectacular 30ft fall, but was held by House who was not anchored at the time. This was one of twelve attempts all of which ended in failure, though in a less spectacular fashion than Ormes'.

Shiprock was finally scaled in October 1939 by Raffi Bedayn, Dave Brown, Bestor Robinson and John Dyer, all members of the Rock-Climbing Section of the Sierra Club, and for the first time expansion bolts of the sort used in the building industry were employed, as well as drills tipped with

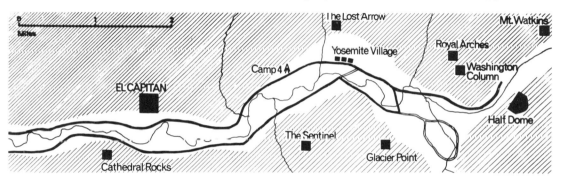

The Yosemite Valley

stellite. In spite of these aids—they did it with four bolts and, of course, also used pitons—it took them three days and part of a fourth, the night of the third day being passed in some discomfort by the four of them in a two-man tent.

One of the most important of the post-war climbers was John Salathé, a middle-aged Swiss wrought-iron worker, with a guttural and picturesquely fractured accent, who lived on fruit. He was an expert in the placing of pitons in cracks that were invisible to others although one of his quoted remarks, 'if a piece of grass can come out a piton can go in', was not always true. He was the first to make pitons from carbon steel instead of iron—for his prototype he used a slice off the rear axle of a Model A Ford—some of his pitons became collector's items.

In August 1946 Salathé made a lone attempt on the Lost Arrow a semi-detached pillar near the Yosemite Falls (lone because his companions failed to turn up) roping down to the Notch, where there was a 1,200ft drop

below him and then, using a drill and his special pitons, climbing about a hundred feet of it to around the halfway point where he left a rock cairn to prove that he had been there. A week later, with John Thune, another member of the Club, he got to 40ft from the top by which time his drill-bits were quite blunted.

Unfortunately, for he deserved to be first on the top, he was beaten to it by a team who succeeded in heaving a weighted line from the rim of the main wall of the valley across the gulf and down over the top of the Arrow.

Salathé's next important climb was the South-West Face of the Half Dome, which could still only be climbed by the route pioneered by George Anderson in 1875. Anderson was a Scot who drilled holes all the way up the face into each of which he inserted an eyebolt. Salathé's companion on this difficult operation was Ax Nelson, a carpenter, also a Sierran. It took them two days and was accomplished with Salathé's pitons. Not a single expanding bolt was used.

Salathé's greatest climb, and one of the greatest of the age, was the Chimney Route on the Lost Arrow which had been turned down by the pre-war climbers as being too much of a good thing.

Besides Salathé and Nelson, two other climbers, Chuck Wilts and Spencer Austin, both South Californians, had already been carrying out reconnaissances and it seemed, from what they had discovered about the climb, that it would take five days. One of the great problems was the heat—in summer the temperature goes up to well over 100°F on the exposed walls of the valley and this meant rapid and serious dehydration unless sufficient water could be carried on the ascent, and enough water meant an enormous extra weight. Salathé's answer to this problem —he was a natural mortifier of the flesh— was to cut the allowance to just over a pint a day—a third or even a quarter of what is today regarded as a normal intake for climbers on the Yosemite wall—and Nelson trained himself to do the same. Salathé also forged what was called a sky hook for the

Yosemite climbing gear: this was the equipment used on the first ascent of Castle Rock Spire (*Climbing in North America*)

operation, an instrument reminiscent of the hooks once used to tear down burning thatch from the roofs of cottages, or haystacks. To save weight, besides cutting their gear and provisions to the bone, they took only one rope, eighteen pitons and twelve karabiners, which meant that one or other of them was regularly employed, like some mad dentist, in descending the face in order to extract the pitons knocked into it at a lower level.

The attack on the Lost Arrow began in the summer of 1947 and both teams continued to make attempts on it all through the hot weather.

Then, once again, Labour Day holiday saw the beginning of an historic and success-ful attempt on a Yosemite wall. On the second day of their climb they succeeded in passing Wilts' and Austin's highest point (it took them two and a half days) and now Salathé was called on to display his talents on a wall of rotting granite in which it was necessary to insert numbers of pitons massed close to one another in order to provide a solid belay. This stretch alone took him eight hours of concentration and pain which began on the afternoon of the second day and continued the following morning after their second bivouac, and it was not until the fifth day that they reached the summit.

Salathé's comment on this great feat, recorded by Nelson and brought to a wider public by Chris Jones in his recently pub-lished *Climbing in North America*, was 'Ve ver pooped out till ve thought ve ver dead'.

The following year, 1948, Salathé, by now nearly fifty-one years old, crowned his career by climbing the North Face of Sentinel Rock (1,500ft) with Al Steck, the first American to climb the North Face of the Cima Grande in the Dolomites by the Comici route. They began their climb over the Fourth of July weekend and on the fifth day, after suffering terribly from the heat, reached the summit. At one stage Salathé was leading for ten hours. It is said that he would never have attempted Sentinel unless Steck had suggested it to him.

The American climber, Tom Frost, starts out under
the roof on the pitch that leads to the headwall,
Salathé Wall (*Climbing in North America*)

El Capitan. The routes from right to left are: Dihedral Wall, Salathé Wall, Muir Wall (*Climbing in North America*)

In 1953 Al Steck, William Siri, Willi Unsoeld and Bill Long climbed El Capitan by the East Buttress and three South Californian teenagers, Royal Robbins, Jerry Gallwas and Don Wilson, all from Los Angeles, climbed the Sentinel with a mixture of free and assisted climbing techniques, knocking three days off the time taken by Salathé and Steck. Robbins had already done some technically very difficult climbs on Tahquitz Rock, a granite peak in South California, but inquiries made by him and the others of local Yosemite climbers and those from San Francisco such as, 'What have you guys got around here worth climbing?' did little to enhance their popularity. Four years later, in June 1957, Robbins, Jerry Gallwas and Mike Sherrick reached the top of the Half Dome by the North-West Face (2,000ft), using angle pitons and ten hard steel pitons made by Gallwas, modelled on Salathé's. It took them five days and was the first Grade VI climb performed on the North American continent.

The most protracted assault up to that time, in the Yosemite Valley, began in July 1957, with a frontal attack on the sheer South Buttress of El Capitan known as the Nose (3,000ft), a wall so smooth and large that even by the mid-fifties no one had seriously considered climbing it.

The protagonists were Warren Harding, a civil engineer with a penchant for driving fast cars, who had been one of the party making the second ascent of Lost Arrow chimney in 1954, Mark Powell who had climbed, among other spectacular spires and needles, together with Gallwas and Wilson, Spider Rock (800ft) in Canyon de Chelly, Arizona, the highest free-standing spire in North America and, most difficult of all, the Totem Pole in Monument Valley on the Utah-Colorado border, as well as a wonderful free climb, with Wally Reed, of the Arrowhead Arête. The party was completed by Bill Feurer, an aircraft engineer.

Great difficulty was experienced in getting to the first proper ledge, 300ft up the wall,

which they called Camp 1. They had to use bolts, although what they really needed were hard steel pitons. Their plan was to establish well stocked camps at intervals up the face, linked by fixed ropes, and the rate of progress was estimated at 100ft a day. From Camp 1 they eventually reached Stoveleg Crack (400ft high), so named because they used pitons made from the sawn-off legs of a gas stove to climb it. After a week on the face, by which time they had a rope up the wall for 1,000ft, they came down.

There was now a long delay until autumn. Owing to the traffic jams brought on by thousands of tourists watching their efforts, the chief ranger banned them from further climbing on the Nose until after Labour Day. When they did get started again Powell broke his ankle. That winter, Feurer, nicknamed the Dolt, evolved some weird and wonderful equipment. One of his memorable bits of gear was known as the 'Dolt cart', made from old aeroplane parts and bicycle wheels which could be loaded with supplies and winched up the face to the camps.

That summer of 1958 they got about halfway up the wall (1,500ft) before the beginning of the tourist season forced them to withdraw once more. Now the team began to break up. Powell was still not fit after his accident the previous year, when he had done most of the leading on the Nose, and now, with newcomers taking an increased part, he finally withdrew.

That September Harding repelled a threat by Robbins to use his ironmongery, still on the face below, to get level with him and then go for the summit with his own party. Harding, with a new team, or rather a succession of climbers, in nine days of terrible heat only managed to climb a couple of hundred feet to a height of 1,900ft on the wall where Camp 4 was set up.

They returned in early November—by this time the climbers were fed up with the Nose of El Capitan—and with Harding and Wayne Merry leading, supported by Rich Calderwood and George Whitmore they forced their

way up through what was called the Great Roof to establish Camp 5 into the region of what was called, in the jargon, the dihedrals, and then Camp 6, by which time Calderwood had given up, leaving Whitmore below, around Camp 4, ready to send up supplies. On 11 November well meaning friends on the rim of the precipice thinking that they were *in extremis* lowered a rope down to them which they rejected. That night Harding, wearing a headlamp, put in twenty-six bolts on the last overhang and at dawn the following day came out over the rim. With various partners he had spent forty-seven days on the face and used 3,000ft of fixed rope, 675 pegs and 125 bolts.

In 1959 the great Teton climber, Yvon Chouinard and Tom Frost, an engineering student at Stamford who was later to take part in the first ascent of the South Face of Annapurna, succeeded in climbing Kat Pinnacle by a new route, the most difficult aided climb in North America. They were enabled to do this because Chouinard like Salathé before him, a great craftsman in ironmongery, had succeeded, using the back of an old truck as a forge, literally on site, in making an amazing new type of piton with a head the thickness of a knife blade which only needed to penetrate $\frac{1}{4}$in into the rock. These Realized Ultimate Reality Pitons (Rurps) were to make climbs possible in the Yosemite without bolts, which up to that time no one had dreamed were attainable.

In 1960 Royal Robbins, Joe Fitschen, Tom Frost and Chuck Pratt, eliminating fixed ropes and using Rurps and Harding's 125 bolts (there could be no retreat) made a continuous attack on the Nose which they reckoned would take them ten days.

The Nose route includes several pendulum manoeuvers [wrote Chris Jones in *Climbing in North America*], and a pendulum is not always reversible. Once they were well up on the wall, there would be only one way to go—upward. A retreat would require the placement of bolt anchors for many rappels down blank sections of the wall. It was an unthinkable prospect. . . . A rescue was not to be considered—there was neither the expertise to carry off a rescue nor sufficient rope on hand to reach down to them from above. In order to cut down the risks they made a pact that they would only rappel with a prusik-knot belay for safety, a precaution they would not normally have taken.

On the afternoon of the seventh day the two teams, who had alternated throughout the attack in leading and hauling, one day each, reached the summit where they were given a great welcome by a big assembly of climbers. In 1969 Tom Bauman made the first solo ascent of the Nose, and in 1971 Robbins led Joanne Marte on the first ascent by a woman.

THE HIMALAYA

16 The Karakoram and the First Attempt on Everest

It is difficult to identify the beginnings of mountaineering in the Himalaya; because to some extent this was always a necessity to its inhabitants, as in any other mountainous zone, and also, because in the nineteenth century it was an essential part of the exploration made in connection with the great Trigonometrical Survey of India, carried out by European surveyors, their skilled native assistants and *khalasis*, unskilled men employed to carry signal poles to summits. Dr Tom Longstaff, one of the great Himalayan climbers of the 1900s, recorded that the world's altitude record was held for twenty-three years by a *khalasi* who carried one of these poles to the summit of Shilla, then thought to be a 23,050ft peak, in the trans-Himalayan Zaskar Range, a record that has naturally attracted dreary attempts to discredit it. Any of these surveyors, none of whom used ice-axes, ropes or pitons, but who carried theodolites, the largest of which, a

12in model, was a two-man load slung on a pole, would have been surprised to have heard themselves described as climbers.

Until 1852 the world's highest mountains were considered to be No XLII in Nepal (Dhaulagiri) at 26,795ft and No VIII in Sikkim (Kangchenjunga) at 28,148ft, according to the calculations at the time. That year, according to a picturesque but untrue story, chief Computer Radhanath Sikhdar, a Bengali, rushed into the office of Lieutenant Andrew Waugh, Sir George Everest's successor as head of the great Trignonometrical Survey of the Himalayan Range. 'Sir, I have just discovered the highest mountain in the world!' It was Peak XV, for which observations by theodolite from six stations had given a mean height of 29,002ft. Thirteen years later Waugh named Peak XV Mount Everest, after his distinguished predecessor. It scarcely matters that the height was subsequently corrected to 29,141ft and later demoted to

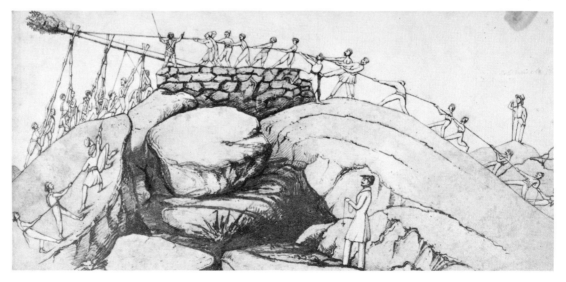

The great Trigonometrical Survey of India by Sir George Everest, Surveyor General of India: the erection of a survey mark about 1832 near Simla. A European assistant in the foreground holds a plumb-line (*India Office Library*)

29,028ft. It *was* the highest mountain in the world—the next highest is K2 in the Karakoram, the latest official height according to the Survey of Pakistan, being 28,741ft.

The first climber to come to the Himalaya for the sake of climbing was a Hungarian, Maurice de Déchy, in 1879. With him came the guide, Andreas Maurer, whose saying was that 'where the clouds can go, men can go; but they must be hardy men'. Unfortunately, de Déchy was taken ill and his plans for what would have been the first climbing expedition of its kind in the Sikkim Himalaya came to nothing.

In 1883 William Woodman Graham, a twenty-four year old climber who, two years previously, had made the first ascent of the highest summit of the Aiguille du Géant became the first visitor to climb in the Himalaya 'more for sport and adventures than for the advancement of scientific knowledge'. With him was Josef Imboden of St Niklaus (near Zermatt). They climbed an unnamed peak of over 20,000ft in Nepal and when Imboden went down with jungle fever and was forced to return to Switzerland, Graham managed to replace him with Ulrich Kaufmann of Grindelwald and Emil Boss who, besides being one of the owners of the famous Gasthof Bär at Grindelwald, was also a fine guide. Together the three men attempted to force the very difficult gorge of the Rishiganga in the Kumaon Himalaya, the only way into the Sanctuary, the basin of Nanda Devi (25,645ft).

Graham's party penetrated as far as the lower reach of the Rishiganga by way of the Dibrugheta, a glen in the outer rampart of the Sanctuary and were the first known men to do so. However, they were unable to force the upper gorge into the Inner Sanctuary, from which Graham had hoped to attack Nanda Devi itself. (The forcing of the gorge—one of the classic mountaineering feats of the thirties—was finally accomplished by Eric Shipton and H. W. (Bill) Tilman with Sherpa porters in 1934, on what was the ninth attempt on it.)

Graham's party then climbed, without much difficulty, according to Graham, what he claimed to be A21, now known as Changabang (22,520ft) on the inner rampart of the Sanctuary, probably another peak on the outer one.

It was now 12 August. By dint of a lot more travelling, by 8 October (again according to Graham), they reached the summit of the colossal Kabru (24,076ft) in the Sikkim Himalaya, by way of the South-East Face, in three days. Doubt has been cast on this climb to an altitude not otherwise reached until many years later, principally because of the short time taken for its completion, but there is no reason to doubt Graham's honesty, only his accuracy—he was no artist with map or compass.

In 1907 two Norwegians, Carl Wilhelm Rubenson and Monrad Aas, both inexperienced mountaineers, spurred on by Graham's alleged feat, succeeded in getting to an estimated 23,900ft, within 180ft of the summit, from a high camp at about 19,500ft, near the foot of the ice-fall on the Kabru Glacier. Together with their Sherpa porters they spent thirteen days and nights at over 19,500ft including three nights at over 21,500ft, without suffering serious deterioration—Aas, however, had his toes badly frostbitten.

One of the great and courageous mountaineering exploits of these early days was the crossing of the 18,000ft Muztagh Pass (*Muz-tagh* means ice mountain), in the Karakoram range, to the Baltoro Glacier. This was accomplished in 1887 by Francis, later Sir Francis, Younghusband, then a twenty-four year old officer in the 1st King's Dragoon Guards. Younghusband, who was working for Intelligence, was on an immense journey which took him from Manchuria to India by way of the Gobi, a desert never crossed before by a European, and a traverse of more than 1,000 miles north of the Hwang-Ho. 'It was nearly midday when we reached the top of the Pass', he wrote in his book *The Heart of a Continent* (1896).

(*Overleaf*) A great early mountaineering feat was the crossing of the 18,000ft Muztagh Pass in the Karakoram range to the Baltoro Glacier, seen here. This was achieved in 1887 by Francis Younghusband, a twenty-four year-old army officer (*Instituto di Fotografia Alpina 'V. Sella'*)

Martin Conway led the first real Himalyan expedition, organised by the Royal, and Royal Geographical, Societies in 1892. It explored the Baltoro, Hispar and Biafo Glaciers (*RGS*)

. . . there was nothing but a sheer precipice. . . . If we could get over, the crowning success of my expedition would be gained. But the thing seemed to me an impossibility. I had no experience of mountain climbing, and I had no ice-axes or other mountaineering appliances with me. I had not even any proper boots. All I had for foot-gear were some native boots of soft leather, without nails and without heels— mere leather stockings. . . . We had brought an ordinary pick-axe with us and Wali (the guide) went on ahead with this, while the rest of us followed one by one behind him in case he slipped while hewing steps across the ice-slope (which was as steep as the roof of a house, and ended in an ice-fall which itself terminated in the head of a glacier at the foot of the pass) . . . and though I tied handkerchiefs, and the men bits of leather and cloth, round the insteps of our smooth native boots, to give us a little grip on the smooth slippery ice, I

could not help feeling that if any one of us had lost his foothold, the rest of us would never have been able to have held him up with the rope, and that in all likelihood the whole party would have been carried away and plunged into the abyss below. . . . At last, just as the sun set, we reached the glacier at the foot.

The first real Himalayan expedition was organised from England by the Royal, and Royal Geographical, Societies. It took place in 1892 and was led by Martin Conway, later Lord Conway of Allington, 'the only eminent mountaineer with whom W. A. B. Coolidge found it impossible to pick a quarrel'. Among its members were Charles Bruce and five Gurkhas from his regiment which had helped to make the expedition possible by the part it had played in controlling the robber barons of the Hunza-Nagir region. With it, too, was the famous Alpine guide, Matthias Zurbriggen of Macugnaga. The party crossed a number of passes in the Karakoram and surveyed and explored the Baltoro, Hispar and Biafo Glaciers, the last two of which combine to form an uninterrupted river of ice 76 miles long.

After climbing Crystal Peak (about 19,400 ft) on 23 August, Conway, with Bruce, Zurbriggen and two Gurkhas, Karbir and Harkbir, made an unsuccessful attempt on Baltoro Kangri (23,390ft), otherwise known as the Golden Throne. They did, however, reach the summit of Pioneer Peak (22,600ft), a minor peak of the Golden Throne group, from which it was separated by an impassable gap. Conway's expedition paved the way for the great expedition of the Duke of Abruzzi in 1909, which found its large-scale maps of the glaciers very useful.

In 1902 the British climber, Oscar Eckenstein, led an expedition to K2. The highest point reached was about 21,500ft on the slopes of an unnamed subsidiary peak (22,380ft) on the North-East Ridge, by Dr V. Wesseley, an Austrian, and Dr Jules Jacot-Guillarmod, a Swiss; but they were unable

K2: Camp 5 of the Duke of the Abruzzi's Karakoram expedition in 1909. The attempt on the summit failed but they reached a reported height that varies from 19,685ft to 22,000ft. The summit, then thought to be 24,783ft is now accepted as 28,741ft (*Instituto di Fotographia Alpina 'V. Sella'*)

to go higher because it was too difficult for the Balti porters.

In 1895, A. F. Mummery, Geoffrey Hastings and Professor J. Norman Collie made a reconnaissance of Nanga Parbat (26,658ft), a peak in the Kashmir Himalaya, the ninth highest in the Himalayan range and one that was to have a particularly disastrous history of fatalities in the course of the next eighty years or so.

During Mummery's expedition, on which

1921 Mount Everest Expedition. Their objective was to reconnoitre a route to the top (*RGS*)

he was joined by Bruce with two of his Gurkhas, they reconnoitred the Rupal Flank, the South Face of the mountain, which rises from the Rupal Nullah to the summit in a wall 14,900ft high.

At this point Bruce was forced to leave the party. Then the weather worsened; Hastings was sent off to get further supplies of food and by 18 August, when Collie, Raghobir Tharpa and Mummery set up an advanced camp on the Diamir Glacier to attempt the North-West Face, Collie was too unwell to continue. The attack on it therefore fell to Mummery and Raghobir who succeeded in reaching a height of about 20,000ft after climbing a difficult rock rib with avalanches pouring down on either side of them. Mummery believed that he could have reached the summit the following day—in fact he would probably have needed at least four properly supplied higher camps on the final 7,000ft—as one distinguished climber, G. O. Dyhrenfurth wrote: 'One is left almost with the impression that Mummery merely tried to transfer to Nanga

Parbat tactics, which had been so successful among the Chamonix Aiguilles.'

On 23 August, Mummery, together with the two Gurkhas, set off to cross from the Diamir Glacier to the Rakhiot Glacier, a depression between the North Summit (Nanga Parbat 2) and Ganalo Peak, to the north west. They were last seen on 24 August, by two porters, who had established a food dump for them in case they had to retreat. They were probably overwhelmed by an avalanche. At the time this melancholy disaster caused as much of a stir as the disappearance of Mallory and Irvine on Everest in the twenties.

The lessons that Bruce learnt from this disastrous expedition, as a leader of future Everest expeditions, was that special food was necessary at 20,000ft and above—Collie had succumbed to a diet that was far too rough for high altitudes—and that it is not possible to rush a 26,000ft peak from 20,000ft. He had also learned that Nanga Parbat was a perilous mountain to trifle with. 'I wonder whether Nanga Parbat will ever be climbed', he wrote. 'At present it seems beyond the strength of man.' It was the last attempt for thirty-seven years.

In 1907 Longstaff, Bruce and A. L. Mumm, a London publisher, one of the first to experiment with the use of oxygen on mountains (which he did that year), made another attempt on Nanda Devi. They had with them Moritz Inderbinen of Zermatt and the two Brocherel brothers of Courmayeur as guides and nine Gurkhas. They failed to break through into the Inner Sanctuary because the Rishiganga was in flood but Longstaff, the Brocherels and Subadar Karbir Burathoki of the Gurkhas succeeded in gaining the 23,360ft summit of Trisul, on the south-west curve of the outer horseshoe, from a camp on the Trisul Glacier at 17,400ft. This was the highest summit so far attained in the Himalaya of which the height was accurately known. The most important conclusion that Longstaff reached as a result of this climb was that the bad effects of remaining at high

Wollaston and Mallory at
21,000ft on the 1921 expedition

altitudes are cumulative.

In 1899, Douglas Freshfield, Professor Edmund Garwood, a geologist who had explored with Conway in Spitsbergen in 1896–7, the Sella brothers and one of the famous, clandestine 'Pundit' explorers employed by the Survey of India, Rinzin Namgyal, made what Freshfield referred to (in his book *Round Kanchenjunga*, 1903) as 'a high level tour' of Kangchenjunga (28,207-ft), a mountain in the Sikkim Himalaya, third highest in the world, which has subsidiary summits, three of them over 26,000ft.

In the course of this reconnaissance Garwood made a much improved map of the mountain and Freshfield came to the conclusion that the innermost corner of the north-north-west side, below the North Saddle at the head of the Kangchenjunga Glacier, was the only practicable direct route to the summit.

The first real attempt to climb it was made in 1905 by a party consisting of, Dr Jacot-Guillarmod, who had been on K2 in 1902,

Alexis A. Pache and Charles A. Reymond, R. de Righi, an Italian, and Aleister Crowley, who had also been on K2 with Jacot-Guillarmod, who asked him to be the leader. It ended in disaster when a whole rope of climbers, six in all, came off the face on a traverse at just below 21,000ft, resulting in the deaths of Packe and his servant and two porters. Crowley, in his tent, took no notice and continued to write an article. Not unnaturally this was his last expedition and from now on he busied himself with demonology as 'the Great Beast'.

1909 was the year of the great Italian expedition to the Karakoram, led by Prince Luigi Amedeo of Savoy, Duke of the Abruzzi, grandson of King Victor Emmanuel II. The Duke, who was then thirty-six years old, already had a great and deserved reputation as a climber and explorer.

He began his climbing career in 1894 and later climbed the Zmutt Ridge of the Matterhorn with Mummery and Collie; in 1897, he made the first winter ascent of Monte Viso and in July of that year made the first ascent of Mount St Elias, the 18,008ft peak in Alaska.

In 1899 he was given command of the Italian expedition which attempted to reach the North Pole from Teplitz Bay in the north of Franz Josef Land. During the winter of 1900–1 his fingers were so badly frostbitten that two of them had to be amputated and the leadership devolved on Lieutenant Umberto Cagni whose party, on 25 April 1901, reached 86.34N, within 220 miles of the Pole, the most northerly point reached at that time. (Cagni, who later became Admiral of the Italian Fleet, had to amputate one of his own frostbitten fingers with a pair of scissors!)

In 1906 the Duke led an Italian expedition to the Ruwenzori, the great mountain massif on the Congo-Uganda border, Ptolemy's 'Mountains of the Moon', long thought to be the source of the Nile. All the principal peaks were climbed.

Among the party was an eminent geographer, Filippo de Filippi, who wrote the account of the expedition; and Vittorio Sella, the greatest mountain photographer of the age, with the possible exception of the Englishman, William Donkin; and seven Italian guides and porters, all from Courmayeur. On 24 May they reached a camp site at what Conway had named Concordia, after the basin of the Aletsch Glacier in the Swiss Oberland—this is the junction of the Godwin-Austen Glacier (named after the man who explored them in 1861), descending from K2 on the north, with the Baltoro and Upper Baltoro Glaciers to the west and east, and with the Vigne Glacier to the south.

From Camp 3, 6 miles up the Godwin-Austen Glacier near the southern foot of K2, it was decided to attack the summit of one of the mountain's six ridges by way of the South-East Rib and Camp 4 was set up at 18,242ft. This attack by the Duke, the three guides, the four porters and a number of Balti coolies carrying their own tents 'and a supply of chupattis', failed at about 22,000ft,

on what was later named the Abruzzi Ridge, because it was too much for the untrained porters.

He now moved his party up the Savoia Glacier which descends from the west ridge of the mountain to the Godwin-Austen Glacier, and on 7 June, from what was now his fifth camp on the mountain, he attacked the West Ridge with his guides.

It took them twelve hours to cut steps up a wall of very steep, hard ice to it. At the watershed (at 21,871ft) they found themselves cut off from the summit of K2.

The north-west, western and south-western approaches had all now been explored and the Duke returned to Camp 3, south of K2, above the junction of the Godwin-Austen and Savoia Glaciers, to make an attack on the North-East Ridge by the route followed by Eckenstein's 1902 expedition. The attack was held up by heavy snow and dangerous avalanche conditions below the Windy Gap (20,450ft) but, on 24 June, Camp 8 was set up at about 21,650ft by the Duke, Joseph and Laurent Petigax and Enrico Brocherel. By this time even the guides, some of whom were iron men, were beginning to feel the effects of altitude. Alessio Brocherel was suffering from a dry, racking cough, Enrico, 'an uncommonly robust man, with the physique of an athlete, was taken with coughing, from no apparent cause, had pains in the breast, and spat blood.'

From this point, at the foot of the South-East Ridge of Skyang Kangri (24,752ft), they were prevented from going any higher by two huge crevasses, the second of which, '20 or 30 feet broad, went all the way across the slope to where the side walls went down right and left into the valley. There was no getting around this obstacle; it formed an absolute barrier to further progress.'

The attempt had failed. All through the month the party had so far spent on the mountain the weather had been appalling. It continued to be terrible but, nevertheless, the Duke now decided to attack Chogolisa,

Conway's Bride Peak, a 25,112ft mountain, south of the Baltoro Glacier.

From a base at Camp 11, at around 16,400ft above the glacier, he succeeded in setting up Camp 14 at a height of 20,784ft, on the Chogolisa Saddle, due east of the peak. It was now 10 July and there had been eight days of dreadful weather. Now, thanks to the efforts of the gallant Balti porters who carried full loads up to Camp 14, he was able to maintain a position there for a further eight days. The health of the party of four was now extremely good and they all slept well at this, and higher altitudes, in spite of being crammed into two small Mummery tents.

On 12 July, wearing first snow-shoes and later crampons, Joseph Petigax, Enrico and Emilio Brocherel and the Duke, having crossed two *bergschrunds* and ascended very steep slopes threatened by avalanches, reached 23,458ft, at which point dense fog compelled them to turn back. By the time they reached Camp 14 it was snowing. None of them had had any serious difficulty in breathing during the ascent.

On the 17th, with the help of the porters, they succeeded in setting up Camp 15A at 22,483ft by their pressure-readings with a Fortin barometer—only 2,627ft below the summit which was then thought to be 24,783ft but is now accepted as 25,110ft. This climb was made in thick snow which had fallen between the 13th and the 16th.

On the morning of 18 July the four men left Camp 15A at 5.30 am. 'The air was lifeless, the sun weak and pale and surrounded by a watery aureole of clouds, a sight of most unfavourable augury.' By now, however, the snow was reasonably compacted and in an hour they had reached the top of the shoulder at 23,000ft, although the mist had again come down.

They knew [Filippi wrote] they had to keep in midway between the cornice [which they had seen on the previous attempt] and a great open crevice a little way below. The snow was very trying, being over two feet deep, and the grade very steep. The foot went down so far at every step that one felt there was no solid ground beneath. At every ominous creaking of the snow they were obliged to bear away obliquely towards the cornice, until the appearance of fissures and the breath of a cold wind from below warned them that they were hanging over the abyss. ... Again they would cut the slope farther down until at no great distance from them an extent of snow would detach itself with a crack and slide rustling down toward the gap. The pickaxes sunk to the handle without meeting any resistance, so there was no hope of their being able to stop the snow from sliding. Nothing could be seen beyond a few yards, but they realised that bottomless gulfs opened on every side.

By 11 am, having climbed for four and a half hours, with short rests every fifteen minutes, they had reached 24,278ft, but it then took them two hours to climb some rocks covered with verglas and while doing so, for the first time, they experienced difficulty in breathing. The fog was still thick but they knew the cornice was to their right and that the mountain side, covered with *séracs*, fell away to the left and there was yet another great, steep snow-slope rising above them into the murk. They were at 24,600ft.

The weather was mild but fog made their situation one of extreme peril. They waited two hours for it to lift, until 3.30 pm when they were forced to retreat in order to avoid being benighted. By the time they reached Camp 15A it was snowing hard; but, nevertheless, with the aid of the waiting porters, they were able to strike it and reach Camp 14 on the saddle at 8 pm, after a day of fourteen and a half hours, at least eleven of which had been spent in climbing between 22,483 and 24,600ft.

The highest point so far reached by man was 24,600ft. If Graham's climb, to a height which he stated was around 23,900ft, with Boss and Kaufmann in 1883 was an authentic one, then it had been exceeded by 700ft. The next highest altitude was supposed to have been reached by the brothers Schlagintweit of Munich, 22,250ft on Kamet in 1855. It was an altitude not exceeded until 1922 when Mallory, Somervell and Norton reached about 26,800ft on Everest. The Duke's camp at 22,483ft was also the highest ever pitched up to that time, although Longstaff had passed a night tentless on the snow crest of Gurla Mandhata in 1905, at a height tentatively estimated by him to be about 23,000ft.

'He and his guides lived', wrote Filippi, 'for thirty-seven days at or above 16,000ft, and then for another seventeen were never below 18,000ft, of which nine were spent at and above 21,000ft—all this under the disadvantage of cramped accommodation, almost constant bad weather and with nourishment reduced from want of appetite'.

In 1920 the Royal Geographical Society and the Alpine Club, sent Colonel Howard Bury to India where Sir Charles Bell, a friend of the 13th Dalai Lama, obtained Tibetan permission for British expeditions to go to Everest. As a result, in May 1921, a party led by Howard Bury and consisting of nine British climbers, including George Mallory and Guy Bullock, and forty Sherpa Bhotia porters, set out from Darjeeling with a hundred mules to discover a route to the top. By 1 July they had sighted the North Col from a height of 19,100ft in the basin of the Rongbuk Glacier and two days later, from a peak on the west side of the Rongbuk Glacier, Mallory and Bullock were able to trace the route that would be attempted from the North Col to the summit—the steep, but not impossibly steep, North Ridge, running up from the col to join the North-East Ridge which leads to the top. On 19 September, after other surveying, including a reconnaissance of the impossible East Face, three Sherpas, Mallory and Bullock finally reached the North Col from the upper basin of the East Rongbuk Glacier where they had set up a wind-blasted, fearfully cold camp. From the col, at a height of 22,916ft, they could see

Members of the 1924 Everest Expedition, without Irvine and Mallory. Back row (*left to right*): Hazard, Hingston, Somervell, Beetham, Shebbeare: front (*left to right*): Bruce, Norton, Noel, Odell (*RGS*)

Bottom right: Guy Bullock on the 1921 expedition. He and Mallory reached the North Col at 22,916ft where they set up a wind-blasted camp. He wears snowshoes (*RGS*)

the long rock- and snow-slopes of the North Face. The scourging west wind of Everest was terrifying, unbelievable. Mallory wrote:

And higher was a more fearsome sight. The powdery fresh snow on the great face of Everest was being swept along in unbroken spindrift and the very ridge where our route lay was marked out to receive its unmitigated fury. We could see the blown snow deflected upwards for a moment where the wind met the ridge, only to rush violently down in a frightful blizzard on the leeward side. To see, in fact, was enough; the wind had settled the question; it would have been folly to go on. . . .

This expedition had accomplished its aim in spite of the heavy September snow—a route at least as far as the North-East Shoulder (about 27,500ft), from which it might be possible to reach the summit; 12,000 square miles of the Everest region had been surveyed and some 600 square miles of terrain to the west had been photo-grammetrically surveyed, albeit fairly primi-tively. A great deal too had been learned about weather conditions and human endurance. As Mallory wrote: 'It might be possible for two men to struggle somehow to the summit . . . the climbers must have above all things good fortune and the greatest good fortune for mountaineers—some constant spirit of kindness in Everest itself.'

Equipped with all the knowledge won by the 1921 reconnaissance party, the 1922 expedition led by the great-hearted General C. G. Bruce, beloved by Tibetan, Sherpa and Gurkha hillmen alike, attacked the mountain by way of the East Rongbuk Glacier and the North Col. On this occasion the highest point reached was 27,300ft below the North-East Ridge, by George Finch and Geoffrey Bruce, both using open-circuit oxygen appa-ratus. It was the highest point so far reached by man. The expedition was later abandoned after an avalanche killed seven Sherpas below the North Col.

The 1924 expedition was led initially by

North Face of Everest and the Rongbuk Glacier (*RGS*)

General Bruce, but when he was taken ill, Edward Norton took over and an assault plan, evolved by Mallory was adopted. Three attempts at the summit were made, Norton himself reaching 28,126ft—the highest point ever reached at the time—only 81ft lower than Kangchenjunga, the third highest mountain in the world. Mallory and Irvine made the third attempt, never to return. No trace of them was found until 1933 when Wyn Harris and Wager found an ice-axe, made by

Willisch of Täsch, in the Swiss Valais, at a height of about 27,600ft, about 60ft below the North-East Ridge, which could have belonged to either of them. One fellow member of the expedition, Odell, who had a last fleeting glimpse of them in the mist, believed they were not roped, had become benighted and then froze to death after, possibly, having reached the summit. Odell himself slept for eleven nights at heights of 23,000ft and more, something that has never

The famous view of Mount Everest with Norton (*left*) at 28,018ft. No photograph had been taken at such a height before (*RGS*)

been done on Everest since. All the climbers that year suffered more or less from a dilated heart condition.

On the five successive British expeditions which attacked the mountain before World War II, no one got any distance beyond the Great Couloir, reached by Norton, which leads up to the final pyramid.

Everest After World War II

Although the great thirteenth Dalai Lama

Shipton and included two New Zealanders, one of whom was Edmund Hillary, a bee-keeper, who had been on one previous Himalayan expedition. Another member was Tom Bourdillon, a physicist, who, together with his father, was to produce the oxygen apparatus used on the successful attack in 1953. This expedition pioneered the route to the West Cwm, the upper basin of the Khumbu Glacier, by way of the difficult and dangerous Ice-Fall.

Mallory and Irvine leave for the final fatal assault on Everest 1924. No trace of them was found until 1933 (*RGS*)

had granted permission to Everest expeditions, this was withdrawn after his death and that approach closed. Nepal, however, opened its frontiers to foreign climbing parties and, in 1949, H. W. Tilman was allowed to lead a small expedition to explore the head-waters of the Trisuli Gandaki, westwards of Annapurna.

In 1951 what was then known as the Joint Everest Committee sent a full-scale British reconnaissance expedition to the south side of Everest in Nepal. It was led by Eric

1952 was the year of the Swiss. Their first party, consisting of eight climbers, three scientists, 165 porters and twenty Sherpas, and led by Dr Wyss-Dunant, was probably the best equipped expedition to attack Everest up to that time. They had extremely light closed-circuit oxygen apparatus, the actual oxygen being carried in special containers which only weighed 2lb, specially constructed climbing suits, isothermic tents and pneumatic sleeping bags which were insulated against the cold.

The climbers were Switzerland's best, the leader being René Dittert with René Aubert, Dr Gabriel Chevalley, Raymond Lambert and nine Sherpas, including Tenzing Norkay, by that time the most experienced climber of his race. He had been on the 1935, 1936 and 1938 Everest expeditions, and on Nanda Devi with the 1951 expedition. As well as being Sirdar of the Sherpas, he was now a full climbing member.

Camp 4 had been established under the West Ridge in the West Cwm (21,150ft), the first time anyone had set foot here. Camp 5 was set up on the Lhotse Glacier (22,630ft), 2,000ft below a rock buttress which divides into a great couloir leading upwards to the ridge between the South Col and Lhotse. The way to the col was up the right hand of this buttress which the Swiss named L'Éperon des Génévois (the Geneva Spur). The plan was to set up Camp 6 at just over 26,000ft at the Col, and Camp 7 at 27,500ft on the South-East Ridge, or higher if possible, and from there to get as close to the summit as they could. Two Sherpas began to suffer from frostbite and were sent down from 25,300ft. A night was spent in great discomfort in two tents below the col, roped together and without sleeping bags. There was a high wind and it was fearfully cold. Nevertheless Tenzing brewed tea and the party of seven had some food. They reached the South Col the following morning about 10 am, having struck camp at sunrise. The west wind was now so strong they could only move on all fours while they pitched their tents and there they remained that day and the succeeding night. The following morning three Sherpas were too exhausted to continue and Lambert, Flory and Aubert continued with Tenzing to a snow-col at 26,300ft and from there to the foot of the South-East, and final, Ridge. Lambert and Tenzing had been using oxygen but it only gave relief when they halted. They were then at 27,300ft and it was Tenzing who suggested they should camp there. Aubert and Flory, it was decided, should turn back, while Lambert and Tenzing pitched their

tent for the night. 'We lay close together slapping and rubbing each other to keep the circulation going', Tenzing wrote afterwards to J. R. Ullman, his biographer. The next day they ascended the ridge for four hours, changing places every twenty yards or so to give the leader a rest from finding the way and cutting steps, encouraging one another with the words 'Ça va bien!' Tenzing recorded that 'When things were good it was "ça va bien" and when they weren't it was "ça va bien" just the same!' But at about 28,200ft they called a final halt. 'We could have gone further', Tenzing wrote, 'We could perhaps have gone to the top. But we could not have come down again.'

Undeterred, the Swiss made a second attempt in the autumn of the same year, 1952. This time Dr Chevalley was the leader with Lambert leading the climbers as Dittert had had to return home. Tenzing was again a member of the climbing party. The film and camera man was Norman Dyhrenfurth, later to lead the American expedition of 1963. Problems arose when it was time to set up a route with steps and fixed ropes up the Great Couloir to the Éperon. This had been not too difficult in the spring but now the Éperon and surrounding slopes were covered with thick snow. By 31 October the task was almost completed and, split up into two parties under Chevalley and Arthur Spöhel with attendant Sherpas, they were testing their Dräger oxygen apparatus when a block of ice detached itself from high up on the Lhotse face and came roaring down the couloir. It missed Spöhel's party but killed Mingma Dorje, one of the best of Chevalley's Sherpas—he himself was saved by his oxygen apparatus which took the blow. At the same time a third rope of Sherpas came off the slope and fell 600ft, without fatal consequences, although all three were put out of action. This catastrophe, which cast a gloom over climbers and Sherpas alike, led to the camps below the South Col being set up much further to the right under Lhotse. The weather now became evil, with strong winds streaming down on the climbers, and it was not until 19 November that Camp 8 was set up on the north side of the col by Lambert, Reiss, Tenzing and the Sherpas. The following day they reached 26,575ft below the South-East Ridge where the wind produced a temperature of −40°F and there the attempt was abandoned. All who took part spoke with awe and horror of the terrible west wind. This autumn attempt had been mounted too late.

These two expeditions, although unsuccessful in themselves, like the ones that went before, did nevertheless provide a great deal of invaluable knowledge which helped in the eventual conquest of Everest.

A pictorial diagram of the 1921 and 1924 routes up Everest. The heights are approximate as the drawing was made very shortly after the 1924 expedition (*Mansell Collection*)

17 The First Ascent of Everest

The British expedition of 1953 had behind it the accumulated experience of ten expeditions and thirty-two years. There was a strong feeling among its members that 1953 would be the last chance for the British to be first on the summit as both the Swiss and the French were already making preparations for attacks on it in 1954 and 1955.

The expedition was planned with military precision and it was led by Colonel John Hunt, a forty-three year old Army officer, then at the Staff College at Camberley. He had climbed his first high Alpine peak at the age of fifteen and before the war had been on several Himalayan expeditions. During the war he had trained troops in snow and mountain warfare and he had also commanded a brigade of the famous 4th Indian Division.

The party consisted of Edmund Hillary, aged thirty-three, the New Zealander who had been on the 1951 reconnaissance of Everest with Shipton; George Lowe, a schoolmaster, aged twenty-eight, also a New Zealander, who had climbed with Hillary in New Zealand; Alfred Gregory, thirty-eight, a director of a Blackpool travel agency, an experienced Alpine climber; Tom Bourdillon, twenty-eight, the physicist who had been on Shipton's reconnaissance, and Charles Evans, a surgeon aged thirty-three, who had been with Tilman in the Annapurna range in 1950. All these had been on Shipton's expedition in 1952, to Cho-Oyu, the world's eighth highest peak (26,750ft). This was a training and acclimatisation operation for the 1953 attempt on Everest, although they failed to reach the summit; and in the course of it Bourdillon had carried out experiments with various sorts of oxygen apparatus. And there was Wilfrid Noyce, a school master and writer with a number of first ascents to his credit, George Band, Michael Westmacott, Charles Wylie, Michael Ward, the expedition's doctor, and the very experienced Tenzing Norkay, again a full member of the climbing team and Sirdar of the Sherpas, now aged thirty-nine.

The equipment was the finest procurable, much of it specially designed for the expedition. With the help of the Polar Research Institute at Cambridge, hooded windproof suits were designed, using material woven from cotton and nylon and lined with nylon, which only weighed $3\frac{3}{4}$lb. Under these the climbers wore another two-piece suit lined with down, a thick cashmere pullover, two featherweight Shetland jerseys, a shirt and woollen underwear.

Great attention was paid to their feet. Four pairs of socks were worn, three woollen pairs and a down outer-sock, and two sorts of boots were taken, one for lower altitudes, the other for the actual attack. The former had double leather uppers specially treated to prevent them freezing—one of the bug-bears of high altitude climbing—and these double uppers were lined with fur (the soles were of treaded rubber, Vibram-type). A pair weighed approximately 3lb 12oz. The high-altitude boots had uppers of thin, glacé kid with an inner waterproof lining, the space between lined with Tropal, a web of kapok fibres.

Altogether a complete climbing outfit weighed about 17lb and was effective down to $-40°$F, the temperature encountered by the Swiss expedition above the South Col.

It was estimated that a climber needed

Mount Everest with South Col on right West Shoulder and the Khumbu Ice-Fall below (*Norman G. Dyhrenfurth*)

The 1953 expedition (*RGS*)

between 5 and 7 pints of liquid a day, plus another ½ pint from the fluid content of cooked food, to make up for water loss caused by the dryness of the air and the increase in the rate of breathing, as well as the loss of fluid in the form of sweat, especially when climbing on glaciers exposed to the sun. According to Griffith Pugh, a physiologist attached to the expedition, sun temperatures of 156°F were recorded on Cho-Oyu at 19,000ft in May 1952.

Three sorts of oxygen equipment were carried: an open-circuit set in which the wearer inhales air enriched with added oxygen, but fitted with a special economiser which had the effect of delivering oxygen during inspiration only, thus avoiding waste.

The closed-circuit set had no opening to the outside air. The climber inhaled a high concentration of oxygen directly from a breathing bag. He exhaled through a soda lime canister which absorbed the expired carbon dioxide and allowed the exhaled oxygen to return to the breathing bag.

The third apparatus was a sleeping set of the open-circuit type which supplied 2 litres of oxygen a minute.

Great importance was naturally paid to providing acceptable food. Pugh and Band wrote:

High up on Everest in 1933 Shipton had a craving for a dozen eggs; Smythe wanted Frankfurters and Sauerkraut; in 1924 Somervell's favourite diet was strawberry jam and condensed milk; on Cho-Oyu Hillary wanted pineapple cubes and Secord wanted tinned salmon. In general, men prefer to eat nothing rather than put up with something that is distasteful to them, and if they do not eat they deteriorate all the more rapidly.

To deal with this problem the assault rations were packed in units consisting of one man's rations for one day.

The expedition left Kathmandu on 10 and 11 March and by 27 March was gathered in the neighbourhood of the Thyangboche Monastery south west of Everest at around 12,000ft, together with 7½ tons of equipment which had been carried there on the backs of 350 porters—ten men alone had been necessary to carry the chests of Nepali coin with which the local people preferred to be paid for their services, rather than with paper money.

Between 6 and 17 April, climbers and Sherpas made trial ascents in the neighbouring region up to an altitude of 20,000ft in order to acclimatise and test out the various sorts of oxygen apparatus. Of a total of thirty-four Sherpas, at least half were expected to go as far as the South Col—and did so. On 13 April the attack on the Ice-Fall was begun by Hillary, Lowe, Band and Westmacott who was in charge of the sectional, alloy, builders' ladders which were used to bridge the crevasses.

Camp 3 was established on 22 April, at the head of the Ice-Fall, (20,200ft); and Camps 5, 6 and 7 between 3 and 17 May, more or less on the route used by the Swiss in their autumn attempt, at 22,000, 23,000 and 24,000ft.

On 20 May, Noyce and eight Sherpas went to Camp 7 to open up the route towards the South Col. This was by way of the couloir up the righthand, southern side of the Éperon des Génévois, the 2,000ft long Geneva Spur which divides the Great Couloir falling from the ridge between the South Col and the summit of Lhotse, the route pioneered by the Swiss in 1952.

On the 21st, in fine weather, but with some wind high up towards the crests, Noyce and Annullu, who had taken part in the Cho-Oyu assault, set off across the Lhotse Face from Camp 7 and by 12.30 pm had reached 25,000ft, where they could be seen to be making a very high traverse that would take them into the Great Couloir near the top of the Éperon. At this time Annullu was leading, 'Moving', according to Noyce, 'at the pace

Two sorts of boots were taken: one for lower altitudes (*right*) with double leather uppers specially treated to prevent freezing, the other (*left*) for high altitudes with thin, glacé kid uppers and a waterproof and kapok lining. Bourdillon puts on the latter (*RGS*)

157

of a fast Alpine Guide', and both men were using oxygen.

It was now that the watchers at Camp 4, Advanced Base, watching through binoculars, realised that they were intending to go to the col itself. Great excitement prevailed. At 2.40 pm the two men reached a point above the col at 26,000ft and from it looked down on the remains of the Swiss camp, where they presently picked up some Vita-wheat, a tin of sardines and a box of matches, and Annullu exchanged his oxygen set for a filled rucksack, before starting the descent. When they returned to Camp 7 at 5.30 pm Noyce said that it had been 'one of the most enjoyable day's mountaineering I've ever had', although both of them were exhausted and suffered from headaches and coughs. So ended a twelve-day struggle to pioneer the way to the col.

The following day, 22 May, after a night of

high wind at Camp 7, Hillary and Tenzing, followed by Wylie and seventeen Sherpas, reached the col with loads which would be used to establish Camps 8 and 9.

On 24 May the First Assault Party, consisting of Bourdillon, Evans, Hunt, Da Namgyal and Balu reached the col in a high wind and there, among the eerie remains of the Swiss camp, they began to set up Camp 8.

My oxygen had finished before descending to the Col [Hunt wrote] and Charles Evans took off his set to leave him more free to work. We were far too weak to compete against the fiendish gale. For over an hour we fought and strove with it [a pyramid tent] . . . trying to put up one single tent which can be put up in one or two minutes lower down.

The night was spent in the pyramid tent and a

From *South Col* by Wilfrid Noyce by permission of William Heinemann Ltd

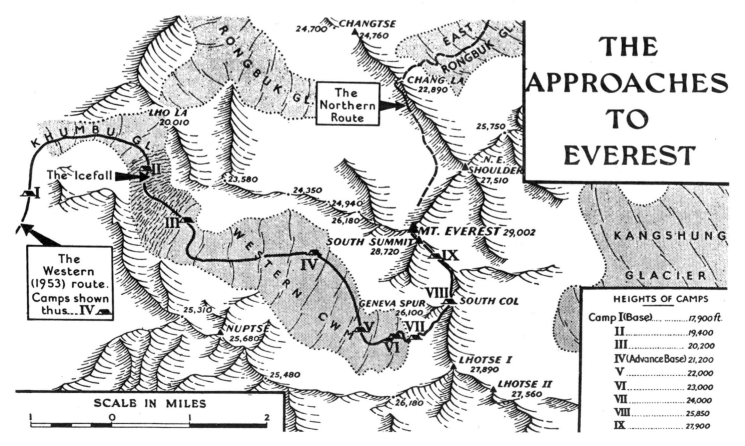

THE APPROACHES TO EVEREST

The Western (1953) route. Camps shown thus...IV

The Northern Route

The Icefall

SCALE IN MILES

HEIGHTS OF CAMPS	
Camp I (Base)	17,900 ft.
II	19,400
III	20,200
IV (Advance Base)	21,200
V	22,000
VI	23,000
VII	24,000
VIII	25,850
IX	27,900

Hillary hacking steps in an ice-fall (*RGS*)

Meade, which was easier to erect. In spite of the terrible wind which streamed over the col they managed to get some sleep with the help of oxygen, having decided to postpone the first assault for twenty-four hours.

The following day, the 25th, they pitched a third tent, a 6lb blister, designed by Campbell Secord, who had originally put forward the idea of the 1951 Reconnaissance to the Himalayan Committee.

On 26 May, Hunt and Da Namgyal, using open-circuit sets, carried stores for the Second Assault Party to 27,350ft on the South-East Ridge, by way of a snow-filled couloir which as the Swiss had found was the only practicable way to it. After passing the remains of the little tent pitched by Lambert

and Tenzing at about 27,300ft—the struts still stood with some scraps of orange cloth fluttering from them—they continued for what seemed to be another 150ft, until they found a space large enough to take a tent. There, after building a cairn, they left a small tent, food, kerosene, oxygen bottles and even a candle and matches.

It was now 11.30 am and they turned back. They had been climbing for four hours.

Meanwhile, Bourdillon and Evans, the First Assault Party, delayed by the valves freezing up on Evans' oxygen apparatus (both men were using closed-circuit sets) had quickly overtaken Hunt and Da Namgyal and reached the South-East Ridge at 9 am. Although climbing at a higher level and

Below left: The Khumbu Ice-Fall. Each month it becomes transformed, fresh surprises occur every few days (*RGS*)

Below right: One way up the icefall (*RGS*)

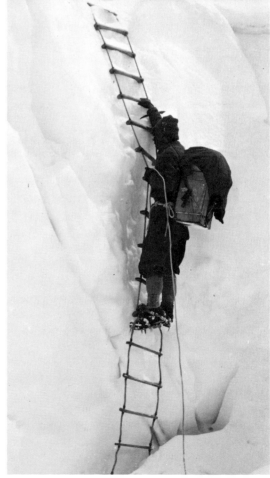

carrying even heavier loads (about 52lb each), they were climbing at a rate of 933ft an hour —at the same time cutting and kicking steps in unbroken snow—against Hunt and Namgyal's 494ft an hour; and by 11 am they had reached Lambert and Tenzing's highest point of 1952 at just over 28,000ft.

There they had to change the soda-lime canisters on their closed-circuit sets, as they were rapidly becoming exhausted. Even when this was done Evans' set continued to give trouble and it was difficult for him to breathe. Nevertheless he carried on and at 1 pm, after climbing over steeply inclined rock and unstable snow, they reached the South Summit of Everest, at over 28,700ft, the highest point so far reached by man.

Although there was cloud all round them at a lower level they could now see the final ridge ahead. It was not prepossessing, being narrow and rising steeply. To the left, its western side, it fell away to the crags above the West Face which itself falls 8,000ft sheer to the West Cwm. To the right, the east, an even steeper precipice fell away, some 9,000ft to the Kangshung Glacier, the East Glacier of Everest in by that time Chinese-occupied territory. This eastern side of the South-East Ridge appeared impassable. 'Huge bulges of snow hung over it from the crest of the ridge, cornices of Himalayan dimensions formed by the westerly wind.'

Time and insufficient oxygen to ensure their return to the South Col decided them, very reluctantly, to retreat. By 4.30 pm, utterly exhausted in mind and body, they reached Camp 8, where Hunt and Da Namgyal had already arrived in a similar condition.

That same day, 26 May, the Second Assault Party consisting of Hillary and Tenzing, supported by Gregory, Lowe, Pemba and Ang Nyima, as well as four more Sherpas carrying extra loads, arrived at the col; while seven Sherpas, including Balu, who had been out of action ever since he arrived at Camp 8, went down to the West Cwm. Meanwhile Ward and Noyce had moved up

to Camp 7 in support of the South Col party. The night of 26–27 May was a particularly horrible one, with a terrific wind roaring over the three tents and very low temperatures. When Hillary lit a match in his tent at 4 am he saw that the thermometer was registering –13°F. Yet, as Hunt recorded in his diary:

For me, this is my third day spent on or above the Col, and I've had three nights of it. But it is interesting to compare our condition with that of the Swiss who spent a similar period here last year, and who scarcely got down alive. Here are we, well supplied with food, fuel and oxygen, sitting at 26,000ft almost as if at Base.

Nonetheless, when Bourdillon, Evans and Ang Temba began the descent on the morning of 27 May, Bourdillon was so ill that he was unable to proceed unaided. Hunt therefore took the difficult decision to abandon his important post at the col as director of the assault and helped to get him down. All were utterly exhausted when they eventually reached Camp 7 and it was fortunate that Ward was there to give medical assistance and Noyce to cook as none of them were able to do this for themselves.

All that day the wind poured over the col, while Hillary, Tenzing, Lowe, Gregory, Ang Nyima and Pemba prepared for what would be for them their last chance to make their attack on the following day.

All through that night of the 27 28th the wind howled on unabated; but in spite of it, breathing oxygen at the rate of a litre a minute, they mostly managed to sleep or at least doze for seven or eight hours.

On the morning of 28 May, with Wylie and three Sherpas now at Camp 7 in support, the wind eased around 8 am and at 8.45 Lowe, Gregory and Ang Nyima, the only Sherpa now fit to climb, Pemba having been ill during the night, set off for the South-East Ridge. Each of them was carrying 40lb, including their open-circuit sets from which they breathed oxygen at 4 litres a minute, and,

climbing at a rate of 430ft an hour, while cutting and kicking steps in snow, they opened up the couloir and the way across to the South-East Ridge.

Hillary and Tenzing left at 10 am. They were also wearing open-circuit sets and each carried a total load of about 50lb. Following in the steps of the first party, and also using oxygen at 4 litres a minute on this section they caught up with them at noon at the Swiss tent, climbing at a rate of 620ft an hour.

Then, with loads augmented from Hunt's dump (50–63lb), they climbed together some 600ft to 27,900ft where it was decided to set up Camp 9.

There, while the others went down to the col, Hillary and Tenzing pitched their tent, using oxygen bottles to anchor the guylines in the soft snow. They did this without using oxygen themselves as by now they only had one and two-thirds bottles each with which to reach the summit and although there were still two bottles, each about one-third full, left by Evans and Bourdillon below the South Summit, Hillary decided that the following day they would have to reduce their intake from 4 to 3 litres a minute.

Later in the evening the wind dropped away and they had a meal of sardines on biscuits, tinned apricots, dates and biscuits with jam and honey, washed down with great quantities of liquid heated over a primus. In spite of their tent being pitched on ledges inclined at an angle of 30 degrees, and a temperature of −16.6°F they had a reasonable night, thanks to their sleeping sets which gave them sufficient oxygen for four hours' sleep each at a litre a minute. When the dawn came, around 4 am, they could see the Thyangboche Monastery below them to the south west.

After drinking quantities of lemon juice and sugar and eating the last of the sardines on biscuits they set off at 6.30 am, each carrying a 30lb oxygen set. By 9 am they had reached the South Summit, at 28,740ft, having found the two oxygen bottles below it, but leaving them there for the return journey. By this

Evans and Bourdillon with their closed circuit oxygen apparatus. When they were on the first assault party they had difficulty with the valves freezing up (*RGS*)

time they had each one 800-litre bottle left, enough for four and a half hours' climbing at the reduced rate and the jettisoning of two empty bottles reduced their loads to 20lb each.

They were now on the final ridge and here were confronted by the huge ice-cornices which had appeared so depressingly formidable to Evans and Bourdillon, and with reason, for in fact they overhung the ridge on either side, above the Kangshung Glacier to the east and the West Cwm.

Fortunately the snow was firm and they were able to traverse below them on the left, although they had to cut steps all the way and were sometimes forced to descend as far as the rock bluffs overhanging the void above the West Cwm. 'It was a great thrill', Hillary wrote, 'to look straight down this enormous rock face and to see, 8,000ft below us, the

tiny tents of Camp 4 in the Western Cwm.'

It was somewhere here that Tenzing began to breathe with difficulty and Hillary discovered that the exhaust pipe of his open-circuit set was frozen up, with icicles depending from it

The weather was perfect, but the wind was bitter. After an hour's climbing they came to a rock step, 40ft high, which spanned the ridge from edge to edge: its face so smooth as to be unclimbable at such an altitude.

The only way up it was by way of a narrow crack, on the right-hand side between the rock and a large ice-cornice which seemed to be on the point of falling to the Kangshung Glacier, now 10,000ft below.

Leaving Tenzing to belay me as best he could [Hillary wrote] I jammed my way

Far left: 'Hillary's Horror' in the Khumbu Ice-Fall (*RGS*)

into this crack, then kicking backwards with my crampons I sank their spikes deep into the frozen snow behind me and levered myself off the ground. Taking advantage of every little rock hold and the force of knee, shoulder and arms I could muster, I literally cramponed backwards up the crack with a fervent prayer that the cornice would remain attached to the rock. Despite the considerable effort involved, my progress although slow was steady, and as Tenzing paid out the rope I inched my way upwards until I could finally reach over the top of the rock and drag myself out of the crack on to a wide ledge. For a few moments I lay regaining my breath and for the first time really felt the fierce determination that nothing now could stop us reaching the top. I took a firm stance on the ledge and signalled to Tenzing to come on up. As I heaved hard on the rope Tenzing wriggled his way up the crack and finally collapsed exhausted at the top like a giant fish when it has just been hauled from the sea after a terrible struggle.

This great effort, at around 29,000ft had come near to breaking both of them; but they went on, flanked by huge cornices.

I had been cutting steps continuously for two hours, and Tenzing too, was moving very slowly. As I chipped steps around still another corner, I wondered rather dully just how long we could keep it up. Our original zest had now quite gone and it was turning more into a grim struggle. I then realised that the ridge ahead, instead of still monotonously rising, now dropped sharply away, and far below I could see the North Col and the Rongbuk Glacier (on the Tibetan side) I looked upwards to see a narrow snow ridge running up to a snowy summit. A few more whacks of the ice-axe in the firm snow and we stood on the top. My initial feelings were of relief—relief that there were no more steps to cut—no more ridges to traverse and no more humps to tantalize us with hopes of success. I looked at Tenzing and in spite of the balaclava, goggles and oxygen mask all encrusted with long icicles that concealed his face, there was no disguising his infectious grin of pure delight as he looked around him. We shook hands and then Tenzing threw his arm around my shoulders and we thumped each other on the back until we were almost breathless. It was 11.30 am. The ridge had taken us two and a half hours, but it seemed like a lifetime.

After he had taken photographs of Tenzing waving his ice-axe embellished with a string of flags (United Nations, British, Nepalese and Indian), Hillary looked out on the fantastic enfilades of peaks, dominated by Makalu (27,824ft), the unexplored, unclimbed giant to the southeast, the fifth highest mountain in the world.

Then, after they had made appropriate offerings to the gods—Tenzing various sweets, Hillary a crucifix given him by Hunt, which they buried together in the snow, and having looked for any signs that Mallory and Irvine might have preceded them there, they left the summit where they had been for fifteen minutes.

By 1 pm they had reached the South Summit where they drank some lemonade. By the time they reached their reserve supply of oxygen, and below it Camp 9, it was 2 pm and they were both very tired. There, while Tenzing brewed a hot, sweet drink, Hillary changed the oxygen cylinders on their sets.

By the time they reached the Swiss high camp a high wind had destroyed all their laboriously cut steps and between them they cut 300ft of steps down hard snow on the Great Couloir before reaching softer going. A couple of hundred feet above the col they were met by Lowe, bringing spare oxygen and hot soup, and just short of the tents Hillary's oxygen ran out. Of the eleven British climbers, nine reached the South Col as did nineteen Sherpas with 30–40lb loads. Six got there twice.

No account of the first ascent of Everest would be complete without this well known picture of Tenzing on the summit. 'In spite of the goggles and oxygen mask all encrusted with long icicles that concealed his face, there was no disguising his infectious grin of pure delight.' (*RGS*)

18 Everest after 1953 and the First Traverse

Of all the post-war attacks on Everest, apart from the first ascent of it, the one that most kindles the imagination is that made by the American Mount Everest Expedition of 1963 which accomplished the first traverse of the mountain, from the hitherto unclimbed West Ridge to the summit, and from the summit to the South Col. It was the first time that one of the great peaks had been climbed simultaneously from two directions.

The leader was Norman Dyhrenfurth, the Swiss-American who had been on the Swiss expedition to Everest in 1952 and the Swiss Dhaulagiri expedition of 1960, on which eight climbers reached the summit at 26,795ft

without oxygen. The deputy leader was William Siri, a biologist and physicist who had led several expeditions: in South America, to Makalu in 1954 and, as field leader, to the Antarctic in 1957–58. Altogether a total of some twenty Americans took part in the expedition, including three doctors and three scientists almost all very experienced climbers —there was also one Englishman, Lieutenant Colonel James Roberts of the Gurkhas, the transport officer who had already been on six Himalayan expeditions in Nepal. The principal backer of this huge enterprise, which cost $400,000, was the National Geographic Society of Washington.

Camp 1 was set up above the icefall in which six days earlier a lump of ice 'about the size of two railroad cars' had fallen and trapped two members of the expedition and killed a third (*Norman G. Dyhrenfurth*)

The advance base, Camp 2, at
21,250ft, with the approaches
to the West Ridge, the frontier
between Tibet and Nepal
(*Maynard Miller*)

On El Capitan in the Yosemite Valley (*John Cleare*)

In September 1962 a rehearsal was held on Mount Rainier in the Cascades Range of Washington D.C.—a complex, 14,950ft mountain with many glaciers which cover an area of 48 square miles, the largest glacier system in North America, outside Alaska. There the equipment was tried out. It included specially designed open-circuit oxygen sets with masks made by a firm which normally produced washing machines, and aluminium-alloy oxygen bottles wound with piano wire which, when charged, weighed 13lb each.

Early in 1963, 500 Sherpa and Khampa porters from the Sola Khumbu region—the Sherpa country—and 400 Tamang porters, organised in nine 'legions', carried 900 loads to Thyangboche in the Imja Valley below the Khumbu Glacier, and for the actual climb Roberts enlisted thirty-seven Sherpas.

Base Camp was set up on 21 March at 17,800ft on the glacier below the Ice-Fall and the following day the attack on it was begun by three climbers Willi Unsoeld, Jim Whittaker and Lute Jerstad, and three Sherpas, Nawang Gombu, Nima Tenzing and Pasang Pemba.

A dump was made on the Ice-Fall at 19,300ft, on the site used by the Indian expeditions of 1960 and 1962 which was reached by way of an almost vertical 30ft pitch of ice-wall.

On 23 March a second party set out to complete the route to the top of the Ice-Fall, consisting of Jake Breitenbach, Dick Pownall, Dr Gilbert Roberts, and two Sherpas, Ang Pemba and Ila Tsering.

At 2 pm, while the party was below the 30ft wall, a huge section of ice, 'about the size of two railroad cars one on top of the other', detached itself and fell on them. It trapped Pownall under a block weighing about half a ton and Ang Pemba was left head downwards beneath it, Breitenbach was swept away.

Roberts and Tsering managed to dig out Pownall, who was relatively unscathed and Pemba, who had a dislocated shoulder, but Breitenbach, who was roped to Pemba, was

buried under a huge mass of snow and ice and his body was never found.

After this disaster a halt was called for some days and it was not until 29 March that the Ice-Fall was finally surmounted and Camp 1 set up between the top of it and an immense crevasse at the foot of the West Cwm, similar to the one that had faced the Swiss in 1952. After this crevasse was bridged Camp 1 was re-sited on a snow-plateau on the far side of it. The architects of this final climb up the Ice-Fall were Unsoeld, Whittaker, Jerstad and Gombu, using C clamps which enabled the climber to ascend by sliding them up the rope.

On 2 April, Camp 2, which was to be the Advanced Base, was set up at 21,350ft in the West Cwm under the West Ridge of Everest which runs about 2½ miles due westwards from the summit, before it changes direction, at a height of 23,639ft, towards the Lho La, a pass from Nepal to Tibet another mile to the west north west. Throughout its length this West Ridge of Everest forms the frontier between Nepal and Tibet and is the watershed between the Khumbu and Rongbuk Glaciers.

From Camp 2, two reconnaissance parties set out: one to establish the 'conventional' route to the summit by way of the Lhotse Glacier and the South Col; the other to attempt to find a route to the West Ridge by way of the West Shoulder, which had never been attempted before. These two parties referred to themselves as South Collars and West Ridgers.

On 3 April, Unsoeld and Barry Bishop, a photographer belonging to the National Geographic Society, climbed to 1,000ft above the Advanced Base towards the West Shoulder, where it met the West Ridge. The Shoulder was still 1,400ft above them and separated from them by very steep ice- and snow-slopes with a few rocks protruding from them.

On 5 April, Bishop and Tom Hornbein succeeded in reaching the West Shoulder (23,500ft) by a series of 35- and 45-degree

Mount Everest. The base camp of the 1963 American Expedition led by Norman Dyhrenfurth (*Norman G. Dyhrenfurth*)

slopes, but not the ridge itself which was still higher.

While the West Ridgers were feeling their way over unknown territory, the South Collars, principally Whittaker, Jerstad, Pownall and Gombu, were forcing their way up towards the Lhotse Face and the South Col. Between 3 and 16 April, with the Sherpas carrying big loads, Camps 3, 4 and 5 (at the South Col), were set up at 22,900, 24,900 and 26,200ft.

On 7 April, the West Ridgers, whose numbers had been depleted by illness—they were now Unsoeld, Hornbein, Bishop and Dave Dingman—established the West Ridge Dump, 1,000ft above Advanced Base, and two days later, together with nine Sherpas under Girmi Dorje, who had been to the summits of Annapurna 4 and Nuptse, they set up a four-man tent at Camp 3A, just below the crest of the West Ridge, at 23,800ft.

The next three days were spent trying to reach a suitable site for Camp 4, which was to be around 24,100ft at the foot of the final 4,000ft pyramid; and on 10 April this team, using oxygen, became the first men to stand on the crest of the West Ridge, at about 24,100ft, where they found themselves enveloped in thick cloud. 'On a reconnaissance', Bishop said, in an aggrieved tone, 'you're supposed to see what you're doing, and we couldn't see a bloody thing.'

At night they also used oxygen in order to sleep, but as Bishop said

... the masks (which were of lightweight polythene) were like flexible aquariums, gathering so much moisture during the night that we felt we were drowning in them. Nevertheless Dave Dingman and I continued to use them during the reconnaissance; but Willi Unsoeld and Tom Hornbein discarded them in favour of just sticking the hoses in their mouths and pretending they were getting oxygen after they fell asleep.

On the following day, the 11th, their patience

was rewarded. From the snow-covered ridge they looked out over a stupendous panorama which no climbers before them had ever seen from this angle: the brown, snowless high plateau of Tibet, the fearful North Face of Everest, that had been the scene of so many British attempts and, immediately below them, the Rongbuk Glacier, while 15 miles to the north, with the help of binoculars, they could see the remains of the Rongbuk Monastery where hospitality had been offered to so many climbers and Sherpas in the past, now a Chinese weather station and military post.

From this point (about 24,100ft) they continued to climb up the north side of the ridge. It was covered with the infamous stone slabs which slope downhill towards the climber, a feature of the north side of Everest, which gives him the impression that he is climbing a steep pitched and very unstable tiled roof. Then, at 24,400ft, the weather thickened and they were forced to descend.

On 12 April at 4 pm, Unsoeld, Hornbein and Bishop (by now Dingman was unfit) reached the prospective site of Camp 4 at 25,100ft, having climbed up the north side of the ridge in what was then Chinese territory. It was a difficult climb.

The slabs were covered with powdered snow, just enough to make it impossible to climb without using crampons, yet insufficient to give them a good foothold wearing them.

The site was that rare thing on Everest, a wide, level snow platform. 'A fairy tale camp-site' Hornbein called it. Bishop said it was 'idyllic'. From it, the West Ridge route to the summit could be seen, soaring ahead of them, with innumerable couloirs running up through the north slopes to the crest. The summit itself was invisible, hidden behind the ramparts of the final pyramid.

On 16 April, four days later, the South Collars reached their objective and were greeted by the sight of the remains of six previous South Col camps—British, Swiss and Indian which together constituted 'the highest junkyard in the world'.

Joe Brown, not mentioned in the narrative of this book but one of the greatest climbers Britain has produced. His achievements range from coastal cliff climbs (in this picture), the crags of Derbyshire and to the Himalaya. His influence has been profound (*John Cleare*)

From now on the weather was bad, with high winds and daily snow; but in spite of it the next ten days were spent in stocking the camps through to Camp 5, at the Col itself. Then, starting on 27 April, the Summit Assault teams began moving up towards the Col.

It was now that a battle began over the West Ridge route; not to climb it but to decide whether or not it should be attempted at all. The principal protagonists were Unsoeld and Hornbein and the two leaders of the Expedition, Dyhrenfurth and Siri who, by this time, believed that two simultaneous attacks by way of the South Col and the West Ridge were beyond their powers, and that priority must be given to getting to the top by the surest route, the South Col.

In the course of this discussion the West Ridgers were offered places on the South Col attack. Bishop accepted, as he was bound to do, because his commission was to take photographs for the National Geographic Society and these would have to include pictures of a summit attempt, Dingman withdrew because he knew that he was not fit enough to tackle the West Ridge. This left Unsoeld and Hornbein, who were joined by Barry Corbet and Al Auten.

By 26 April the Sherpas had put seventeen loads on the col; but there were still fifteen more to go up before the summit attack could be mounted.

Meanwhile the West Ridgers, now almost an unofficial body, with as many Sherpas as they could find to help in their seemingly hopeless attempt, were trying to set up winches at Camp 3 to haul loads up from the West Ridge Dump to the camp, a vertical distance of 3,000ft, on makeshift sledges. Two of the winches were hand-operated, the third was a motor winch which operated, when it did operate, on an exotic mixture of rocket fuel.

Corbet's log-book recorded some of the difficulties encountered.

First day: Up from A. B. (Advanced Base) with borrowed Sherpas carrying loads to 3W. Tough 11-hour day. Only two Sherpas stay with us . . . Second Day: Dig winch site. Then take cable hundreds of feet down to dump, put skis together into a sled, place loads and self on sled and give signal for up. Slowly, about 8 feet a minute, sled jerks its way up 30-degree slope— then dies. After interminable wait Al finally calls down that winch starter is broken. Climb back up. . . . Third day: Fight to compress huge coil spring which controls starter rewind. Time after time Al and I get four hands on it, pushing and poking to make it lie flat, and every time, out it comes like a jack-in-the-box. All this in below-zero temperature and high wind, with snow tearing by in a ground blizzard.

This continued until the sixth day, when he wrote: 'Winches won't start. Al and I down to Advance Base. Goddam'.

The motor winch never functioned again and a fully loaded sled hung 500ft below it. Thereafter they tried the hand winches, a back-breaking job at such an altitude.

On 30 April, the first assault party, consisting of Whittaker and Gombu, and Dyhrenfurth and Ang Dawa, reached Camp 5 at the South Col. Below them was the second party, Jerstad and Pownall and Bishop and Girmi Dorje. Lower down too were Dingman and Barry Prather who were to make an attempt on Lhotse, the 27,923ft peak south of the col, first climbed by Ernst Reiss and Fritz Luchsinger on 18 May 1956 on the Swiss Expedition which also reached the summit of Everest (the second climb). They failed to reach the summit.

On 30 April, the First Assault Team managed to establish Camp 6 at 27,450ft, following the route from the South Col used by the British and all subsequent expeditions. This was just short of the Camp 9 used by Hillary and Tenzing, but above Lambert and Tenzing's Camp 7 (above 8,230m) on the first Swiss attack in 1952.

The 'smoke' from an avalanche that has just come off the walls of Nuptse at the base camp (*Maynard Miller*)

Hornbein's snow-filled couloir. This was the way up to Camp 5 from which Hornbein and Unsoeld were to make the final assault (*Barry Corbet*)

The weather was awful, with low temperatures and very high winds, and a crisis developed there when all but one of the eight Sherpas who had carried to this height refused to go down without oxygen, as had been planned. The exception was Dawa Tenzing.

This created a serious shortage of oxygen at Camp 6 which nearly had fatal consequences for the climbers involved in reaching the summit.

That night the wind still continued very strong and lightning was seen. In spite of this all four men, Whittaker and Gombu, Dyhrenfurth and Ang Dawa, slept fairly well with the aid of oxygen and, in the case of the Americans, barbiturates, which were used by most of the high climbers.

The following morning, 1 May, was as bad as it could be for an attempt on the summit—high winds, bitter cold and a huge white plume streaming off the summit. Whittaker, a giant of 6ft 5in, and Gombu, his companion, 5ft 5in, left for their attempt at 6.15 am and by 8 am they were just below the South Summit of Everest at 28,741ft.

At this point they each cached one of their two oxygen cylinders in order to have a reserve on the descent. It proved to be a wise thing to do. An hour later Dyhrenfurth and Ang Dawa left Camp 6 (at 7.15 am) carrying movie equipment with which Dyhrenfurth was hoping to photograph the attack; but at 11.30 am, when they were at about 28,200ft, their oxygen ran out and in spite of Ang Dawa's pleas that they should continue—'Up go, Burra Sahib'—Dyhrenfurth insisted that they should go back from what would almost certainly have been for them a one-way trip.

At that moment, 11.30 am, Whittaker and Gombu reached the South Summit at 28,750-ft, the highest point reached by the Indian Expedition in 1962, also in very bad weather, and from it descended a difficult pitch of 30ft to a saddle. From there the South-East Ridge continued inexorably upwards, in its final section before the summit. It was flanked by the great ice- and snow-cornices which overhang it on either side, to the east, above the Kangshung Glacier in Tibet and to the west above the West Cwm in Nepal, between 10,000 and 8,000ft below, and which had proved so difficult to Hillary and Tenzing.

The last real obstacle that they expected to encounter was a 40ft high, almost smooth, rock to the top of which, in 1953, the year of the successful British Expedition, there had been only one way. This was Hillary's Chimney, an exceedingly disagreeable crack between the rock with an ice-cornice insecurely attached to it above the Kangshung Glacier. Fortunately however, this rock was now silted up with snow and ice on its south side and gave them little trouble.

Above it they struggled on over a succession of humps and hummocks, but by now the ridge had levelled out and beyond the last of the obstacles was the white dome of the summit.

'You first', said Whittaker to Gombu.
'No, you', said Gombu.

Then, the dome being wide enough, they walked side by side to its top. Beyond everything fell away. And there they were. It was 1 pm. 'I slapped Gombu on the back', Whittaker said. 'We hugged each other. I dug my ice-axe in and slung my pack over it. It was windy, very cold, and my fingers and toes were numb.'

The temperature was around $-22°$F. They set up a 4ft aluminium stake with flags flying from it of the US, Nepal, India, United Nations, NGS and the flag of Gombu's Himalayan Institute of Mountaineering in Darjeeling). Then they took photographs. The weather was clear, the view stupendous, except to the north east where the great Everest plume, formed from the snow beneath their feet, streamed away. In all they remained there for twenty minutes, without oxygen, for that was exhausted.

Now began the terrible, oxygenless retreat. By the time they reached the near side of the

Unsoeld and Hornbein reach
the West Ridge. The summit is
barely visible. They had to
remove their overboots and
crampons to negotiate the
knife-edge of the crest that lies
before them (*Norman G.
Dyhrenfurth*)

When asked how he had felt at the summit Whittaker said, 'like a frail human being'.

The West Ridge attempt was now officially on; and on 15 May Camp 4 was finally established at 25,100ft below what was known as Hornbein's Couloir, the route which was to be followed up the north side of the ridge. This couloir had been reached by Unsoeld and Hornbein, two days previously. It was at 26,200ft, the same height as the South Col.

On the night of 16 May a wind of hurricane force at Camp 4 carried two linked tents, containing Corbet, Auten and four Sherpas, 150ft down the north slopes of the ridge towards a 6,000ft drop to the Rongbuk Glacier where they lodged upside down. Hornbein and Unsoeld in their small tent heard nothing of this, which was not surprising in a wind that was gusting at 100 mph; and it was Auten who, having succeeded in pinning the remains down (the others had to remain inside as ballast in order to avoid it being whisked away), then climbed the hundred or so vertical feet to Camp 4 to give the alarm. All three men then went down together in the darkness to belay the tents with ropes. When they had accomplished this almost impossible task they returned to Camp 4, leaving Corbet and the Sherpas to see the night through in the tents which were still upside down.

The next day, after they had already been informed of this catastrophe by walkie-talkie, the listeners at Advanced Base received another message to say that the small tent containing Hornbein, Unsoeld and Auten was also on its way over the edge, the wind being so strong that it lifted the occupants bodily off the ground. They managed to stop it but in the process it collapsed.

There was nothing to be done now but evacuate Camp 4, something which three of the Sherpas in the tents below had already done and that afternoon they reached Camp 3 after an appalling journey, having lost three tents, oxygen masks, sleeping bags and personal gear—Corbet had even contrived to lose all the money he had with him in

South Summit it seemed that they could never make the effort to climb the nearly sheer, 30ft to it, having by now been two hours without oxygen, and the whole day since setting out, without liquid—the contents of their canteens were frozen.

Once beyond it they were able to retrieve their two oxygen bottles from the cache and switch on again, but by the time they reached Camp 6; where Dyhrenfurth and Ang Dawa were waiting for them, they could scarcely speak.

It was now too late to think of going down to a lower camp, as Hillary and Tenzing had done, so all four spent another vile night at Camp 6, before dragging themselves down to the South Col the following morning.

On the way to it they met the Second Assault Party, Jerstad and Pownall and Bishop and Girmi Dorje, who were on their way to Camp 6 and by this time their condition was so bad that the second party had to abandon their attempt in order to shepherd them down.

Nepal which, for some obscure reason, he had on him.

Between 18 and 20 May, the party of South Collars which would be supporting the West Ridgers began to move up to the South Col and on the 21st they occupied it. By this time (on the 20th) the West Ridgers —Unsoeld, Hornbein, Corbet, Auten and Dick Emerson—who had previously been at Camp 3 when the tents blew away, re-occupied Camp 4, together with their five Sherpas, Ang Dorje, Ila Tsering, Tenzing Nindra, Pasang Tendi and Tenzing Gyaltso, only one of whom, Ang Dorje, was an experienced climber.

On the 21st they set off for Camp 5, climbing in three separated teams: Corbet and Auten leading (their job was to find a way up the Hornbein Couloir and a site for Camp 5); then the Sherpas to stock it; then Unsoeld and Hornbein to make the final assault on the summit. Emerson, who was climbing with these two, was only there for the hell of it and when he reached the foot of the couloir, he went no further.

From the foot of the couloir which was snow-filled, Corbet and Auten kicked and cut thousands of steps up it, hour after hour, until, around 2 pm, they found a suitable site for Camp 5, a small snow-platform large enough to take a two-man tent at the foot of the infamous Yellow Band which had been such a curse to the British on the North Face. This band of schist, a substance remarkable for its rottenness, encircles the mountain at around 27,200ft to a height of about a 1,000ft, and is very visible on the North Face below the final pyramid.

As soon as Unsoeld and Hornbein and the Sherpas had come up, everyone except the Assault Party withdrew down the couloir to Camp 4, a major climbing feat, with Corbet acting as anchor man, while Unsoeld and Hornbein pitched their tent and had a good meal which included chicken noodle soup and shrimp with curry.

That same day, 21 May, Jerstad and Barry Bishop, with the help of Pemba Tenzing and Nima Tenzing, reached Camp 6 on the other side of the mountain where they found the two tents still standing from the previous attack. There, Jerstad had a bad night, suffering from lack of oxygen and claustrophobia; but worse was to follow.

At 4.30 am on 22 May they began to prepare breakfast and while they were doing so a butane cylinder caught fire singeing them, completely destroying Bishop's plastic oxygen mask and filling the tent, in imminent danger of going up in flames, with thick smoke. It took them three hours to prepare another breakfast and get themselves in order and it was not until 8 am that they left Camp 6 for the summit in brilliant sunshine. By this time Dave Dingman and two Sherpas, Girmi Dorje and Nima Dorje, had set off from Camp 5 at the South Col for Camp 6 to give support.

At 7 am on 22 May Unsoeld and Hornbein, the two West Ridgers left Camp 5, after having slept until 4 am, when their supply of oxygen for the night ran out.

With loads weighing 40lb, which included two oxygen bottles each, they continued up the Hornbein Couloir through the Yellow Band. Both men's apparatus was to some extent defective and Hornbein, who was number two on the rope, found great difficulty in breathing as his set was only delivering 2 litres of oxygen, in spite of the regulator being set for 3.

By 11 am, four hours after setting out, they had reached 27,750ft, 500ft above Camp 5, and at this point the couloir closed in so that they now found themselves climbing up rock slabs inclined towards them and covered with snow as substantial as flour.

Hornbein now took the lead on what was to be a 60ft pitch. It took him to the bottom of a vertical slab which he was unable to negotiate in spite of having succeeded in driving a piton into the crumbling yellow schist below it. An attempt to reach out beyond the couloir on the exposed North Face failed and they were forced to return to the couloir for a second try at it.

Tom Hornbein and Willi Unsoeld back at base camp after their ordeal of bivouacking overnight on the South-East Ridge in a sub-zero temperature (*Norman G. Dyhrenfurth*)

This time Unsoeld succeeded in getting beyond the slab, but only by removing his gloves and climbing bare-handed and they now reached a relatively more easy part of it, at around 28,000ft.

From here they forced their way up through the last of the terrible Yellow Band on to an open expanse of limestone rock and snow, with no inkling in which direction the summit lay.

It was now 3 pm and they were at 28,200ft. Using their walkie-talkie they called up Whittaker at Advanced Base and told him of their dilemma. No one there could tell them what to do; neither could they communicate with Jerstad and Bishop, with the mass of the mountain intervening.

Jerstad and Bishop had, in fact, reached the South Summit at 2 pm, where a 60 mph wind was blowing, and some time after 3 pm they had reached and passed Hillary's Chimney. At 3.30 pm they were at the summit where Whittaker's and Gombu's monument, the aluminium flag-pole, still stood with Old Glory flying from it. There, they turned off their oxygen and began taking photographs— Bishop was not a National Geographic Society photographer for nothing.

By 4.15 pm, with the sun declining, they were very worried about Unsoeld and Hornbein of whom there was no sign. They began the descent to Camp 6, after having been three-quarters of an hour at the summit.

Unsoeld and Hornbein were in a difficult situation. It was 3 pm. They were unsure where the summit lay; but were equally uncertain of their capacity to descend the couloir. 'It was a most revolting prospect', Hornbein said later. To Whittaker they said that they were going on.

Their decision was the right one. As they climbed above the Yellow Band the prospect opened out and they were able to get their bearings from the position of the glaciers below.

By 4 pm they were at 28,400ft, with the summit directly above them, beyond a great expanse of snow and now, after a late lunch, they moved in to the right towards the West Ridge, with the wind becoming stronger as they climbed towards it out of relative shelter.

By the time they gained the ridge it was 5 pm and now, both using their second and final oxygen bottles, they followed it up with the North-West Ridge of Everest to their left front, the upper basin of the Rongbuk Glacier below on their left flank and the head of the West Cwm below them to their right.

The crest then became such a knife-edge that the rocks could not hold the snow and they had to remove their overboots and crampons in order to negotiate it, putting them on again when they reached deeper snow.

Finally, at 6.15 pm, they saw ahead of them, forty feet or so away, the flagstaff with the flag streaming from it, standing on what, from this point on the West Ridge, was a real summit peak, to which they now climbed. They too had made it after twelve hours of almost continuous climbing. They spent fifteen minutes on the summit taking photographs in the freezing wind. Then, after depositing on it a crucifix belonging to Unsoeld, which he wrapped in a *kata*, a Buddhist scarf belonging to Gombu, and two prayer flags from the West-Ridge Sherpas, they began the long descent of the South-East Ridge towards Camp 6, two hours behind Jerstad and Bishop.

The two parties did not meet until 9.30 pm, 350ft below the South Summit, and the next part of the descent was a nightmare, the South Collars being, if possible, more tired than the West Ridgers. At one point, Jerstad slipped on the knife-edge and would have slipped down to the Kangshung Glacier but for being held by the others' rope. By midnight they were off the knife-edge but they had only descended 400 vertical feet in two and a half hours. It was clearly impossible to reach Camp 6 that night and they continued to make history by bivouacking at 28,000ft on a rock outcrop on the South-East Ridge of Everest without tents, oxygen (by then all exhausted), sleeping bags, food or drink. Fortunately God was kind to them: there was no wind although the temperature fell to $-0.4°F$. Otherwise they would have surely frozen to death.

Hornbein alone had the energy to remove his crampons, which conducted the cold to his feet, but it was his companion, Unsoeld, who insisted he removed his boots and put his feet close to his (Unsoeld's) stomach, not realising that his own feet were already frozen. After five and a half hours of this misery, when the dawn had crept over the world below them with indescribable splendour, they went on down. When they met Nima Dorje and the other Sherpa at Camp 6, they were given huge quantities of liquid which was all that they craved. Everyone had frost-bitten fingers—Bishop eventually lost all his toes and the tops of his little fingers. Unsoeld all his toes but one. As James Ramsay Ullman who accompanied the expedition as chronicler wrote: 'They paid a stiff price for standing, each for his few minutes, on the summit of Everest. ... Was it worth it? The final answer must be their own, not anyone else's.'

19 Nanga Parbat

A. F. Mummery met his death on Nanga Parbat in 1895 and no further attempt was made until 1932 when the Germans began a long series of attacks which continued for the next twenty-one years.

The section which concerns us here lies to the east of the main summit, the East Ridge, running out to the Rakhiot Peak (23,210ft) above the great avalanche-swept glacier of the same name.

In 1932, Willy Merkl, a thirty-two year old Bavarian, and one of the great climbers of the Munich school, led a German-American attempt on the peak, with a group which included one American, Rand Herron of New York (later killed when he slipped on a pebble while climbing the Chephren Pyramid at Gizeh near Cairo). Although they failed at 22,800ft on the East Ridge where Camp 7

Willy Merkl led two attempts on Nanga Parbat in 1932 and 1934. He was one of the great climbers of the Munich school. On the second expedition terrible weather forced them back and he and his six companions including three Sherpas died on the East Ridge (*German Himalayan Foundation*)

was set up, they had at least found the way to the summit.

Merkl renewed his attack with an Austro-German expedition in 1934, but this attempt was soon clouded by the death, from pneumonia, of one of the team, Alfred Drexel. Further disaster struck after Camp 8 had been established on the Silbersattel, a plateau on the East Ridge at 24,500ft. From here two climbers, Peter Aschenbrenner, an Austrian guide, and Erwin Schneider reached 25,280ft below the main summit. In the course of the subsequent retreat during a blizzard, Sherpas Dakshi and Nima Nurbu, Merkl, Gaylay, his personal Sherpa, Uli Wieland, and Willy Welzenbach all died on the East Ridge, while Nima Tashi, Nima Dorje and Pintso Nurbu all died short of Camp 5, either in the snow or frozen to death on the fixed ropes on the Rakhiot Peak. The last survivor to reach Camp 4 from the upper part of the mountain was Ang Tsering, Merkl's second orderly.

From below in Camp 4 [Fritz Bechtold wrote in *Nanga Parbat Adventure*] a man was seen pressing forward along the level saddle. Now and again the storm bore down a cry for help ... completely exhausted and suffering from terrible frostbite ... with almost superhuman endurance, he had fought his way down through storm and snow. Since he brought no letter from Merkl or Gaylay, his simple tale was news of the heroic struggle of our comrades and their faithful porters high on the ridge above.

So ended the greatest mountaineering disaster of our time.

Despite these setbacks, three more German expeditions were mounted before the war. In 1937 a colossal avalanche fell on Camp 4 from the Rakhiot Peak destroying seven Europeans and nine Sherpas. In 1938 no one succeeded in reaching the Silbersattel because of bad weather, but the body of Pintso Nurbu, who died in 1934 on the fixed ropes, and also those of Merkl and Gaylay who had succeeded in crawling 400yd from their last bivouac were discovered. In 1939 an attempt was made by a small party, led by Peter Aufschnaiter of Kitzbühel, to climb the incredibly dangerous North-West Face from the Diamir Glacier, first attempted by Mummery in 1895, with only three porters. They failed at about 19,700ft and were interned in India when war broke out. One of the party was Heinrich Harrer. He escaped to Tibet and became a close friend of the Dalai Lama.

Nanga Parbat was finally climbed in the same year as Everest, 1953, by an Austro-German expedition organised by the much criticised Dr Karl M. Herrligkoffer, the step-brother of Willy Merkl, but not himself a climber. The deputed leader was Peter Aschenbrenner, now over fifty, who had been on the mountain with Merkl in 1932 and 1934. For political reasons, it proved impossible to get entry permits for the seven Sherpas who had been engaged for the expedition and instead they used seventeen men sent by the Mir of Hunza.

The attack was made by the Rakhiot Glacier, on which an ill conceived British expedition had lost two of its members a few years previously, and by 18 June Camp 4 had been established below the slope of the Rakhiot Peak, on the site of the one-time Camp 5, at 21,950ft.

On 25 June news was received that the monsoon was approaching. There had already been heavy snow on the 22nd and 23rd. By this time one of the climbers, Kuno Rainer of Innsbruck, had had to be evacuated from Camp 4 because he was suffering from phlebitis. Aschenbrenner who, as custodian

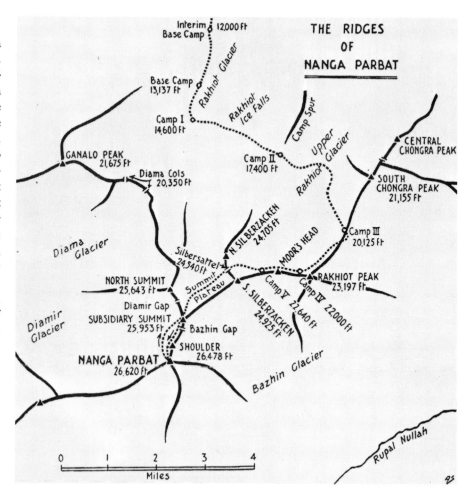

of a hut in the Alps, only had a limited amount of time at his disposal, and had never wanted to lead the expedition anyway, now had to return to Europe.

Before doing so, because the monsoon was imminent, and no doubt with memories of the ghastly results of disregarding its arrival, as in 1934, he ordered the retreat.

Fortunately, as it turned out, although it might have ended very differently, he was disobeyed by the senior member of the party which was then at Camp 4. Walter Frauenberger, an Austrian judge, ignored the repeated radio instructions to descend, although some of them may have emanated from Dr Herrligkoffer.

Eventually they all stayed where they were, and at midday on 30 June the weather cleared. Two days later Camp 5 was established on

From *Nanga Parbat Pilgrimage* by Hermann Buhl by permission of Hodder & Stoughton Ltd

the East Ridge beyond the Moor's Head rock at about 22,700ft, by Frauenberger, Hermann Buhl of Innsbruck, Otto Kempter and Hans Ertl of Munich, and three Hunzas, Ali Madad, Hadji Beg and Hidyat Khan. It was chiefly thanks to Frauenberger, whom the Hunzas called 'the Good Sahib', that the porters were persuaded to climb to this height. Buhl and Kempter then prepared for the attack the following day.

On the next morning of 3 July Buhl, an Austrian climber famous for his solo climbs

Nanga Parbat. The Silbersattel is the ridge running down to the left of the smaller peak. Rakhiot Peak is on the extreme left. This picture was taken on the 1938 expedition (*German Himalayan Foundation*)

and winter routes, set off carrying ski sticks at 2.30 am by the light of the stars and a crescent moon. He was supposed to have been accompanied by Otto Kempter, who had the provisions; but Kempter did not set off until half an hour later—he was still tired, having done most of the step-cutting on a very hard traverse below the Rakhiot Peak on 27 June—and Buhl made the whole of the subsequent climb with very little food.

Although suffering at the high altitude,

Buhl was over the Silbersattel (about 24,500 ft) by 7 am, and the weather was perfect. An hour later Kempter also reached it and was able to see Buhl, a pinprick on the now fearfully hot and blazing white snow-plateau, a mile or so ahead.

At 25,000ft Kempter halted, slept for a while, and then, at about 5 pm, descended to Camp 5.

At about 25,950ft Buhl cached his rucksack with a little food and a pullover, and began to traverse the Vorgipfel (preliminary summit) to the Bazhin Gap—some 670ft higher than anyone had been before on Nanga Parbat and about 700ft below the summit.

This gap in the North-West Ridge was the one which Mummery had tried so hard to reach in 1895 from the Diamir Glacier.

It was now 2 pm and with a thousand feet still to climb, Buhl took two Pervitin tablets, the sort used in the war by German pilots to keep them awake. This would have beneficial effects for between six and seven hours.

A steep rocky ridge crowded with snow towers, vertical pitches of sharp-edged granite, badly exposed cornices and steep flanks of compressed snow, now lay between me and the shoulder, [he wrote]. . . . At this point the mountain-face plunged in a vertical drop of several miles direct from the ridge. . . . Never had I seen such an abyss.

This was the great South Face, the Rupal Flank, which falls 14,900ft to the Rupal Valley. The next part of the climb, to the Shoulder (about 26,300ft), was by the hanging traverse of a gendarme (tower) which Buhl rated at between the fourth and fifth grades of Alpine severity.

I took a last gulp of coca-tea, [Buhl wrote], which offered some fleeting refreshment. Then I traversed into the northern face. Steep and rough, a tumbled mass of boulders now led up to the summit, still about 300ft above me. I now left the ski-sticks behind and—I could do it in no other way—scrambled up on all fours. Suddenly I realised that I could go no higher. . . . I was on the summit.

It was about 7 pm, and the temperature was falling rapidly. He was only there about ten minutes taking the ritualistic but, in this case, important photographs to prove without any doubt that he had been there, then, after hoisting the flags of the Tyrol and Pakistan on his ice-axe, which he left behind in the

excitement of the moment, he began what could easily have been his last descent. Almost immediately he lost the strap of one of his crampons, and now had nothing to support him except two ski-sticks. Indeed, at this moment, if any climber ever was, Buhl was in the approaches to death's dark vale.

With one crampon tied on with string, it took him about two hours to descend 450ft. At about 9 pm night closed in and he spent the next seven hours leaning against a rock in the highest open-air bivouac ever made by

On the Rakhiot Glacier en route from Camp 1 to Camp 2 (*J. F. Lehmanns Verlag*)

The attack on Nanga Parbat was made by the Rakhiot Glacier, below the Rakhiot Peak, shown here. It was below this peak that Otto Kempter cut steps on a very hard traverse (*Paul Bauer*)

man at the time, at over 26,000ft—perhaps only saved from frostbite by the Padutin pills Dr Herrligkoffer had insisted that he should take with him, which stimulated the circulation. Mercifully, it was a calm night for he was wearing only a wind-jacket, a thin pullover and fur-lined boots. It was not until 4 am on 4 July that the moon reached the part of the ridge on which he was standing and he was able to continue the descent—by now his feet were without sensation.

It took him until noon that day, eight hours, to reach what was known as the Diamir Gap (about 25,300ft), by traversing below the Vorgipfel. By this time he was becoming light-headed.

Before me lay once more the vast sweep of the Silver Plateau [the Silbersattel] I could no longer swallow or speak. Blood-stained saliva oozed from my mouth. I longed to get at my rucksack, for hunger was torturing me no less than thirst. . . . It was some time before I could locate the ruck-sack, then finally I fell down beside it. I could not swallow dry food but I made myself a wonderfully refreshing concoction of Dextro-energen and snow and after a prolonged rest I began to feel better again.

Plagued by cruel hallucinations which confused rocks with members of the expedition coming to succour—'Oh, the joy of it. Someone was coming! I heard voices, too calling my name'—Buhl staggered on down the long descent to the Silbersattel with his right foot frost-bitten and a crampon held on by string which kept coming loose.

I would struggle along for twenty or thirty yards then once more would I be fettered and held in total collapse. Two or three steps demanded ten rapid gasps of breath, then twenty, then still more, until eventually I could go on no longer. Then would follow another long rest and the agony would start again.

At 5.30 pm that evening, with the aid of another dose of Pervitin, Buhl reached the Silbersattel. From it, away towards the Moor's Head, the graveyard of Merkl and the others who died with him, after forty hours on the mountain, he saw two men, Ertl and Frauenberger, who really were coming to succour him.

'The sight of them gave me fresh impetus and, as though buoyed up anew by some secret force, I went ahead with greater ease.'

Four years later, in 1957, he was killed on Chogolisa in the Karakoram.

Hermann Buhl on his return from his lone ascent. He was one of the most notable post-war German climbers, noted for his winter and solo ascents in the Dolomites and elsewhere. He was killed while descending from Chogolisa in 1957 (*J. F. Lehmanns Verlag*)

187

The North-East Face of Nanga
Parbat seen from the Rakhiot
Glacier (*J. F. Lehmanns Verlag*)

20 Annapurna

The first peak over 26,248ft in the world to be climbed was Annapurna (26,545ft) in the central section of the Nepal Himalaya, which is separated from another even higher peak, Dhaulagiri (26,795ft), by the gorge of the Kali Gandaki.

Unlike Nanga Parbat, for example, which has a record of exploration going back to the 1850s, little or nothing was known about the peaks in the Nepal Himalaya, with the exception of Everest, before World War II. Indeed, neither Dhaulagiri nor Annapurna had been seen or photographed, except from a great distance, until 1949, when Dr Arnold Heim carried out an aerial photographic reconnaissance on behalf of the Swiss Foundation for Alpine Research.

In 1950 the Himalayan Committee of the French Alpine Club, inspired by these photographs, succeeded in obtaining permission for an expedition to Central Nepal, and it was decided that the objectives would be either Dhaulagiri I or Annapurna I. The principal architect of the enterprise was Lucien Devies, President of, among other mountaineering organisations, the French Alpine Club. One of the difficulties in planning and carrying out the attempt was the absence of accurate maps.

The party was led by Maurice Herzog, an engineer from Chamonix and a very fine climber. With him went three great Chamonix guide-instructors, Louis Lachenal of Annecy, Lionel Terray of Grenoble and Gaston Rébuffat of Marseilles. The other two members of the actual climbing party were Marcel Schatz and Jean Couzy. There were no scientists except the expedition doctor, Jacques Oudot. With them they had some first-class Sherpas: Ang Tharkay, Dawa Thondup, Ang Dawa IV, Ang Tsering III, otherwise known as 'Pansy', Ajeeba, Aila Sarki and Phu Tharkay.

Only three weeks could be spared for the reconnaissance of the east and north-east sides of Dhaulagiri and the approaches to Annapurna, and on 21 April two reconnaissances were begun from Tukucha, a village 8,000ft up, at the point where the Kali Gandaki river breaks through the Great Himalaya. The next three weeks or so were spent in exploration of unknown territory rather than mountaineering. In the course of them all attempts to reach the North-East and South-East Ridges of Dhaulagiri failed, but sufficient was discovered about the North Face to convince the climbers that it was impossible. It was now 14 May, however, and a reconnaissance had been made by Dr Oudot, together with Schatz, Couzy and some Sherpas, which took them above the impassable gorges of a river named Miristi Khola to the foot of the glacier below the North-West Spur of Annapurna. They had found the way to the summit.

There was no time to be lost, with only about a month to go, perhaps less, before the monsoon broke over Nepal. The latest report, on 14 May from the Indian Meteorological Office, was that it would break around 8 June, only three weeks away. Four days later, on 18 May, the expedition had already set up its base camp at 15,000ft at the foot of the North Annapurna Glacier.

From it a reconnaissance by Terray and Lachenal, who together had made the second successful attack on the Eigerwand, reached 19,000ft on the North-West Spur. The weather was very bad, with much snow and

Annapurna, the North Face, first climbed by Maurice Herzog's expedition in 1950, then the highest ascent achieved in the world (*Maurice Ichac*)

ice on the rocks, and the highest point reached by 21 May was about 19,700ft with an almost infinite open-ended prospect higher up.

Accordingly a Base Camp was set up on the glacier at a point about 16,700ft below an ice-fall and all the expedition's forces were brought up from Tukucha. In rapid succession Camps 2, 3 and 4 were established at 19,300, 21,000 and 22,600ft. The first of these was at the foot of the face, while Camp 3 was in a crevasse at the head of a technically very difficult slope of over 70 degrees with vertical steps between, which needed ice-pitons and fixed ropes to open it up. Some 700ft of this fearful route, in constant use by porters and climbers after 31 May when it was established, was a chute down which avalanches poured daily as soon as the sun was high enough to warm the snow that had fallen the previous night.

By this time, although the weather was better on the mountain, Terray and Rébuffat were not fit to try for the summit and neither were Schatz and Couzy. With the monsoon only a few days away—it was reported to have already reached Calcutta—the task of establishing Camp 5, the last high camp before the summit, fell on Herzog and Lachenal. The site, a rock rib at about 24,600ft below the subsidiary East Peak, had already been decided at Camp 1.

On 1 June, with the help of Ang Tharkay and Aila Sarki, setting off from Camp 3, they took a tent from Camp 4 and pitched an intermediary Camp 4A on top of the Sickle, a great concave precipice above the glacier, overhung by the lip of the summit ice-cap. There, the two Frenchmen spent the night.

The following day, 2 June, with great difficulty, and with the help of their porters, who had brought up another tent from Camp 4, moving up over deep snow and slopes swept by avalanches, they reached the site of what was supposed to be Camp 5. There they found it was impossible to pitch a tent, because of the steepness of the slope. As it was, the four of them had to excavate a

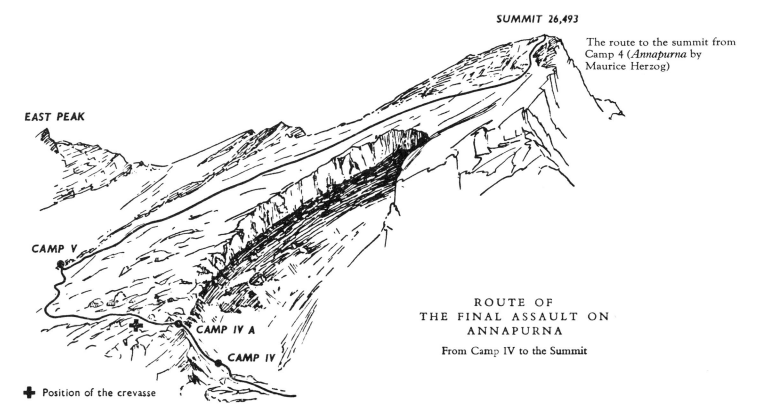

SUMMIT 26,493

The route to the summit from Camp 4 (*Annapurna* by Maurice Herzog)

EAST PEAK

CAMP V

CAMP IV A

CAMP IV

ROUTE OF
THE FINAL ASSAULT ON
ANNAPURNA

From Camp IV to the Summit

✚ Position of the crevasse

platform for it, and literally nail the tent to a rock with a piton to prevent it from glissading down over the edge of the Sickle.

Meanwhile Schatz and Couzy moved up to Camp 4A with Ang Dawa and Phu Tharkay, and Terray and Rébuffat, together with 'Pansy' and Aila Sarki, having carried supplies to Camp 3, struck one of the tents there and took it to Camp 4A. There were now four Frenchmen and four porters at Camp 4A in support of Herzog and Lachenal and Camp 3 was well stocked.

The night of 2 June at Camp 5, on the side of the enormous slope leading to the summit, was a stormy and an uncomfortable one for Herzog and Lachenal; but the following morning was fine although very cold. At 6 am they started out but didn't take a rope. 'That was two pounds saved', Herzog wrote.

The climb to the summit was south-westwards up the enormous tilted expanse of the North-East Face. Each man was 'locked within himself, consumed with sombre thoughts'. What worried both of them was

the sensation of approaching frost-bite. At one point Lachenal asked what Herzog would do if he himself turned back.

'I should go on by myself', Herzog replied. 'I would go alone. If he wished to go down it was not for me to stop him. He must make his own choice freely', he wrote later. Lachenal agreed to follow him.

The die was cast. I was no longer anxious. I shouldered my responsibility. Nothing could stop us now from getting to the top. The psychological atmosphere changed with these few words, and we went forward now as brothers.

The final stretch was by way of a steep couloir up through a rock band, which was filled with good, hard snow. The question was, had they the strength to climb it?

By kicking steps we were able to manage, thanks to our crampons. A false move would have been fatal. There was no need

191

Louis Lachenal on return to camp after the terrible descent when he fell through a crust of snow into a crevasse, fortunately only 15ft deep (*Marcel Ichac*)

to make handholds—our axes, driven in as far as possible, served us for an anchor . . . lifting our eyes occasionally from the slope we saw the couloir opening out on to well, we didn't quite know, probably a ridge. But where was the top—left or right? Stopping at every step, leaning on our axes, we tried to recover our breath and to calm down our hearts, which were thumping as though they would burst. . . . A slight detour to the left, a few more steps —the summit ridge came gradually nearer —a few rocks to avoid. We dragged our-selves up. Could we possibly be there? Yes!

A fierce and savage wind tore at us.

We were on top of Annapurna. . . .

Our hearts overflowed with unspeakable happiness. . . . The summit was a corniced crest of ice, and the precipices on the far side, which plunged vertically down be-neath us, were terrifying, unfathomable. There could be few other mountains in the world like this. Clouds floated half-way down, concealing the gentle, fertile valley of Pokhara, 23,000ft below. Above us there was nothing.

It was 2 pm.

On the descent things began to go against them. Herzog lost his gloves and his mind was too benumbed by the cold and the alti-tude to remember that he had a spare pair of socks in his sack, which would have protected his hands to some extent. The weather, too, changed and soon the two men were en-veloped in thick, swirling cloud and a freezing wind rose. It seemed that the monsoon was finally upon them.

By this time they were separated. Lachenal was well ahead and eventually became in-visible somewhere in the murk below. By the time Herzog reached Camp 5 first, in what was now a blizzard, both hands were frost-bitten, 'violet and white and as hard as wood'. Fortunately for him and Lachenal, Terray and Rébuffat had come up to Camp 5, bringing another tent with them.

Soon after Herzog reached the camp cries for help were heard from Lachenal. He had fallen down the steep face 300ft or so below the camp and had lost his axe, cap, gloves and one crampon. When Terray reached him, with great difficulty as he had forgotten to put his crampons on, Lachenal was, not unnatur-ally, possessed by fear of frostbite and the possibility that some of his limbs might have to be amputated, so that when Terray told him that it was impossible to get down to the base camp in such weather, he tried to wrench Terray's ice-axe from him to go down alone.

All through that terrible night, with the blizzard howling round the tents, Rébuffat and Terray continued to massage Herzog and Lachenal, in an endeavour to bring back life to their marble-like limbs, every so often re-filling the cooking pots with snow to provide drinks for them until, at last, life began to return to Lachenal's toes. Herzog's fingers and toes, however, seemed beyond redemption. The following morning the retreat began: with Lachenal wearing Terray's boots, two sizes larger than his own, and Terray cramming his feet into Lachenal's which he was only able to do because he had had to cut them off him the previous night.

All through that day the four men worked their way down through the ice above the lip of the Sickle in search of Camp 4A, where Couzy, Schatz and four of the Sherpas were well situated, believing the others to be safely at Camp 5.

Then, with dusk coming on and the blizzard still blowing with fearful violence, Lachenal fell through a crust of snow into a crevasse. Fortunately, it was only about 15ft deep and offered far more protection from the elements than the cave which they had been about to excavate as a bivouac; and in it, with only one sleeping bag into which all four stuffed their bootless feet, they passed a terrible night.

Towards morning, snow began to slide into the crevasse, burying them, and they had to fight their way to the surface with nothing

At the summit Herzog had 'fumbled feverishly' in his sack and took out the little French flag and the pennants and his camera, tying the flag to his ice-axe—'useless gestures no doubt but something more than symbols' (*Herzog*)

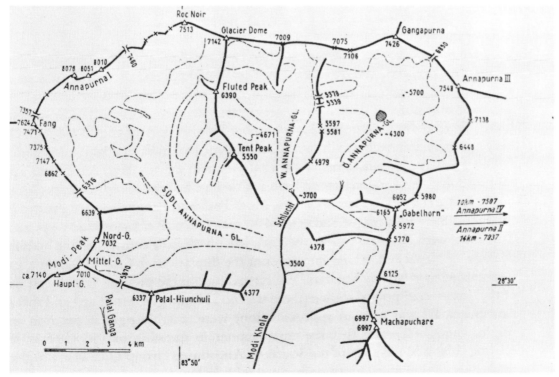

Annapurna and the surrounding peaks (*The Mountain World 1966/67*)

Terray (*centre*) and Rébuffat became totally blind, having failed to wear their goggles. Lachenal is on the extreme right, both men accompanied by Sherpas (*Marcel Ichac*)

on their feet but their socks.

By this time Terray and Rébuffat were totally blind, having failed to put on their goggles the previous day, forgetting the intensity of ultra-violet light on an ice-field even in blizzard conditions; it was the blind but immensely strong Terray who hauled Herzog and Lachenal out of the crevasse.

The blizzard had died away and it was now a fine, sunny morning. There, a little later, when their fate seemed sealed, they were found by Schatz, who had come up from 4A which was quite close.

The descent from 4A to Camp 2, where Dr Oudot was based, by six Frenchmen, two of them blind and two crippled, and six Sherpas all roped and descending steep and hazardous slopes, was a nightmare.

Just above Camp 3, at about 12.15 pm, an avalanche began in the couloir down which they were moving and Herzog and his two Sherpas, Aila Sarki and 'Pansy' were swept 500ft down the mountain towards Camp 2.

By another of the miracles operating on Annapurna that summer—which would never have happened on Nanga Parbat—they all survived.

Now, Camp 2 became an operating theatre at 20,000ft, with Dr Oudot working by torch-light and with amateur assistants to try to save the limbs of Herzog and Lachenal. The next part of their ordeal was an heroic portage by Sherpas who carried them in baskets and on their backs over moraine, through torrents in spate and bamboo thickets. Over the worst of this route the strongest and most enduring of these porters, Pandi, otherwise known as the Chinaman, carried the 14-stone Herzog on his shoulders. The result of their efforts, and those of the devoted Dr Oudot, who had to carry out further trimming of their limbs on a train in India, was that Herzog was fortunate to escape with the loss of his fingers and toes, Lachenal his toes alone. So ended this brave, historic but melancholy expedition.

After the descent Camp 2
became an operating theatre, Dr
Oudot working by torchlight
to save the limbs of Herzog
and Lachenal. Both were then
carried on improvised stretchers,
Pandi, one of the toughest of
the Sherpas, bearing the
14-stone Herzog on his
shoulders (*Marcel Ichac*)

21 Annapurna the South Face

After the successful French attack on Annapurna in 1950, eleven years passed before Annapurna II, III and IV, the other three big peaks in the massif, were finally conquered.

In 1970 Chris Bonington decided to attack the summit by way of the South Face (12,000ft). That same year a German party set up an attack on the South Face of Nanga Parbat, the Rupal Flank (14,900ft), one of the highest mountain walls in the world. It was successfully led by Reinhold Messner, a Tyrolean famous for his solo climbs, who was followed to the summit by his brother, Gunther. Gunther was taken ill and Reinhold made the bold decision to attempt the descent by the little known and unclimbed Diamirai Face to the west. It was carried out without a rope and, near the base of the mountain, Gunther was killed by an avalanche.

By 1970 the conquest of major peaks in the Himalaya had reached the same stage that had been reached in the Alps after the ascent of the Matterhorn in 1865, and climbers were bending their minds to more hazardous routes—ridges and great walls—as technique and equipment evolved. Chris Bonington was one such mountaineer. A leading British climber, he had covered the world from Patagonia and the Eigerwand to Annapurna 2 and Nuptse above the West Cwm of Everest. He and Martin Boysen, another leading British climber, had their first sight of Annapurna's South Face projected from a transparency in Bonington's living room. 'It was like four Alpine faces piled one on top of the other', he wrote, '. . . hard, uncompromising'.

The team he assembled for this extremely hazardous operation consisted of Boysen, Nick Estcourt, Dougal Haston (acclaimed as one of the finest climbers in the world, later to die tragically, killed by an avalanche while ski-ing in 1977), Ian Clough, Michael Burke and Don Whillans, all of whom had climbed with him before, and Tom Frost, one of America's greatest rock-climbers. Six Sherpas were engaged to help establish the higher camps.

For an attack on a 12,000ft snow- and ice-face, much of it sheer or almost so and swept by snow avalanches, a great load of special equipment had to be carried. With them they had oxygen which was not used on the summit attack, 27,000ft of rope, hundreds of pitons and karabiners, winches, ladders, snow-anchors, and twenty-one tents, including six Whillans Boxes with metal frames which could be slotted into a ledge on a steep snow slope. They also had large numbers of Jumar clamps. These *ascendeurs* could be fitted over a fixed rope and allowed the climber, while harnessed to it, to climb the rope by sliding the clamp up it which gripped it under tension.

After establishing Camp 1, at about 16,000ft, by 7 April, in spite of heavy snow and frequent avalanches, Whillans and Haston succeeded in reaching the Col at the head of the Snow Ridge on the lower part of the wall which reminded Bonington of the buttress of a Gothic cathedral. This was at the foot of the great, knife-edged Ice Ridge covered with fragile spires which led up to a band of ice cliffs. Here, at the col, on April 13, at a height of 20,100ft, 2,500ft above Camp 2, Camp 3, a Whillans Box, was set up under an overhang; and in it that night Bonington and

The South Face of Annapurna. A climber can just be seen at the top of the huge cornice of the ice ridge (*left centre*) at 21,500ft (*Chris Bonington*)

Frost listened with awe to snow avalanches thundering down within feet of their 6½ x 4ft wide habitation.

By 18 April, using fixed ropes and Jumar clamps to bring up supplies, only 1,000ft had been gained on the Ridge in eleven days; and on 21 July, after two days in which they only advanced 100ft, Whillans and Haston reached the site of Camp 4 at 21,300ft, another Whillans Box, which was set up three days later, three weeks and 1,200ft above the Col. 'Above,' wrote Bonington, 'the crest of the

Ridge was barred by a series of towers that looked like a jumble of ice-cream cornets that had overflowed their cones.'

On 24 April Boysen and Estcourt began what Boysen later described as one of the most difficult climbs he had ever experienced. It began in an ice tunnel 20ft long and 2ft high which ran clean through the ridge, 'like pot-holing in a deep freeze'. When Boysen, who was leading, stuck his head out at the far end he looked down a 3,000ft sheer ice-wall to the glacier below—the 'Terrible Traverse'.

One of the climbers on an ice bulge: 'the crest of the ridge was barred by a series of towers that looked like a jumble of ice-cream cornets that had overflowed.' (*Chris Bonington*)

He then launched himself on the face of an ice-tower, setting up runners for the rope which was attached to a piton at the far end of the tunnel and cutting hand and footholds above the void on a traverse to the corner of it, and it took him two hours to turn it.

The next part of the pitch was in a 55-degree snow-filled gully 50ft beyond his last belay, followed by a traverse to one side to find ice hard enough to take the next piton. From the crest, having already used up 150ft of rope, he let down another to Estcourt, but

the vertical cliffs. By this time exhaustion was beginning to manifest itself among those using fixed ropes and clamps to carry supplies up the face. Their objective was the Flatiron, a prominent rock spur which took its name from a similar one on the Eigerwand and the way to it was up a 50-degree buttress overlaid with ice and a series of ice-fields and rock walls bombarded by falling rocks that Frost called 'high whistlers.' On 12 May they were driven down by a terrible blizzard but on 14 May they reached it after Burke had led

Ian Clough inside the Whillans box, one of six taken on the expedition. Its metal frames could be slotted into a ledge on a steep snow slope (*Chris Bonington*)

this hung far out from the face because of the cornice and it took Estcourt two hours to come up as he was unable to use Jumars.

It is impossible to follow them throughout their various struggles on the Ice Ridge but, by the third evening (April 27), they were only about 380ft above Camp 4 and it was not until May 5 that Camp 5 was established at the head of the Ice Ridge under some vertical ice-cliffs, after five weeks on it at a height of 22,750ft.

On 9 May Burke and Frost began their attempt on the Rock Band which lay above

the most difficult stretch of rock encountered on the mountain and now Bonington had to take the unpopular decisions as leader that Whillans and Haston then at Camp 3 should force the route from now on and attack the summit.

On 19 May Whillans, Haston and Boysen established Camp 6 at 24,000ft on the crest of the Flatiron by which time Boysen was suffering from lacerations and blood poisoning received on the 'Terrible Traverse'. Here, Whillans spent the night alone because Haston, having dropped his sack with all his

Above Camp 4, 21,300ft. A climber can just be seen well above and to the left of the track in the snow (*Chris Bonington*)

personal gear in it over the edge of Anna-purna, had gone down for more. Then, on 20 May, the same day that a British Army expedition reached the summit by the French route on the North Face, they managed to climb 400ft up a gully in the Rock Band.

That day Bonington, although not fit, set off to Camp 6 with a radio and, what was more important, 500ft of rope, without which Whillans and Haston could go no higher, but was forced to leave the rope 300ft below it. It was then that Whillans who had returned with Haston from the Rock Band still short of the top of it by some 200ft of rope, sug-gested to Bonington that he should help to establish Camp 7. 'I was tremendously moved', he wrote. 'Without thinking I agreed.'

On 21 May, Whillans and Haston, having once been driven back by a blizzard suc-ceeded, later in the morning, with Boning-ton's rope, in making an ascending traverse to the foot of a chimney at the head of the gully at the top of the Rock Band. That morning, Haston wrote, 'The snow was coming down the gully like a raging highland torrent.'

Bonington returned to Camp 5 and made a brave climb to Camp 6 on the 23rd, carrying a colossal load of 60lb, but eventually only managed half-way and that day Whillans and Haston were pinned down at Camp 6 without food or a tent with which to establish Camp 7.

The following day (the 24th) they felt was the crucial one. It was the coldest either of them could remember anywhere in the Alps or the Himalaya. Some delay was experienced in starting up the chimney because, as Whillans said, 'I had to take me boots off to warm me feet'.

Haston began on the chimney. By now they had only about 300ft of rope left and for ironmongery some pegs and about half a dozen karabiners. They then climbed to the head of the chimney, with Haston 'swim-ming' up it in snow until their 300ft of rope was finished, and the two of them then going on past a chockstone (a stone jammed in a crack) unroped—because there wasn't any—to emerge from the Rock Band on an easy snow field with the East Summit, but not the summit of Annapurna, visible. It was a great piece of courageous mountain-eering.

On 25 May, after a night in which they suffered badly from sore throats, it was again intensely cold. In spite of a terrible blizzard they succeeded in producing a 300ft run-out of rope to the top of the gully before being forced back. 'I had gone fifty feet when I could barely see any more', Haston wrote. 'Goggles were ripped off in a rage but then I found my eyelids freezing solid. . . . There was only one thought and that was to reach the end of the gulley and pitch Camp 7.

Back at Camp 6 Bonington and Clough were waiting for them, having carried up food from Camp 5.

'Somehow we packed in out of the storm', Haston wrote. 'Ian [Clough] was bent double in the far corner. Don and Chris facing each other with legs bent and intertwined. I was in an icy pool at the door.' All through 26 May the blizzard raged. That morning Bonington and Clough went down. 'The summit', Haston wrote, 'was once again beginning to fade into the vague future. We were alone with our sombre thoughts and the wind.'

The following day was the same; only brightened by news over the radio that a carry of food was being organised from a dump between Camps 4 and 5 at the top of the Ice Ridge.

The morning of 27 May was not good, but nothing like as bad as the preceding ones. They left at 7 am and by 11 am were on the ice-field at the head of the gulley. With them they had a 10lb nylon tent, but after discuss-ing the alternatives Whillans said, 'I think we should press on and find a camp site as close to the final wall as possible'. It was a great risk and they took it. With Whillans leading and Haston carrying the tent and rope, they went up the ice-field towards a nasty-looking snow-ridge, with an 800ft face above it.

At the ridge Haston jettisoned the tent.

Haston (*left*) and Bonington in a snowhole like the one Bonington and Clough 'packed' into out of the storm at Camp 5 (*Chris Bonington*)

'Time was pressing and there seemed no point in taking belays', he wrote. He makes it sound like an afternoon's outing on a horizontal snow-filled meadow, not a climb at 26,000ft on something more nearly approaching the vertical. By this time Haston was having trouble with the strap of one of his crampons which came off three times on the final wall. As a result Whillans was about 100ft ahead of him. Then he disappeared over the edge of the summit ridge. Haston wrote:

The final fifty feet needed care. Big flat unsolid snowy rocks which had to be scraped clean. Over the ridge and suddenly it was calm. There was no wind on the north side. . . . Don was already fixing a rappel peg. We didn't speak. There was no elation. The mind was still too wound up to allow such feelings to enter. Besides the supreme concentration was needed to get down. The real problem was the actual summit. We were on a ridge. The snow peak to the left looked highest so Don plodded up the thirty feet or so to its top

while I filmed the historic moment Vague traces of what must have been army footprints showed beneath the snow. The view was disappointing. . . . The greatest moment of both our climbing careers and there was only a kind of numbness. . . . Meanwhile there was still the face to climb down. Fortunately I had carried up a hundred and fifty feet of rope in my pack so the hardest section could be bypassed by abseiling. That was our summit monument. A fixed rope. It seemed appropriate as it was the last fifteen thousand feet of such.

Whillans and Haston survived the descent unscathed. That evening of 27 May Bonington called them up at Camp 6 on the radio and asked Haston if they managed to get out that day. 'Aye', said Haston, 'We've just climbed Annapurna.'

Since this great climb there have been others equally worthy of record, but everything has to have an end . . .

Ian Clough on the Terrible Traverse, set up by Boysen who described it as one of the most difficult climbs he had ever experienced (*Chris Bonington*)

Acknowledgements

In writing this book I became conscious, as anyone must who is dealing with history, of the difficulty, if not impossibility, of avoiding errors of fact. Some will be of my own compounding; others because the source material is either exiguous or itself open to question. I can only apologise in advance to the reader if 5 March should have been 6 March, or south east south west, or 3,250m 3,150m. Heights indeed are among the most common sources of error and dispute in mountaineering literature, being liable to continual change as new surveys are made. Mistakes also frequently occur when heights in feet are converted into metres or vice versa. In this book it was thought best to aim for consistency within chapters. In those dealing with Europe metres have been generally used, for the Himalaya, the Americas and New Zealand, feet. Even so, this did not avoid the sort of problem exemplified in the chapter on the climbing of the Matterhorn. Here Whymper has to be quoted as saying (for this is what he wrote): 'The Matterhorn was ours! Nothing but 200ft of easy snow remained to be surmounted.'

In connection with these problems I would like to take this opportunity of extending my heartfelt thanks to Mr D. F. O. Dangar, a past assistant Editor of the *Alpine Journal* for the enthusiasm and energy with which he devoted himself to a meticulous examination of the manuscript and proofs. I also wish to thank Anne-Marie Ehrlich, our picture researcher, for the patience she showed in tracking down illustrations for the book and Christine Kirk for her really beautiful typing of a manuscript which looked as if it had been crawled over by a horde of centipedes whose feet had been dipped in ink. And I wish to thank James MacGibbon of David & Charles: his enthusiasm for the book, and patience, far exceeded that normally displayed by an editor. Also the staffs of the Alpine Club, the London Library and the Royal Geographical Society for their indefatigable assistance. Finally among all the books listed in the bibliography which I consulted in the course of writing the book two must be singled out as having been of especial value: Walt Unsworth's *Encyclopaedia of Mountaineering* (Robert Hale, London; St Martin's Press, New York) without which I would have not known how to begin and Chris Jones' recently published and excellent *Climbing in North America* (University of California Press) to which I am totally indebted for the chapter on the Yosemite and the climbers of Southern California.

Bibliography

Abney, W. de W. and Cunningham, C. D. *Pioneers of the Alps* (1887)
   Alaska and the Yukon (Hachette World Guides)
   Alpine Journal, The, especially Centennial volume, 1957. Alpine Club, London
   American Alpine Journal, The
Baedeker, K. Various guides to European Alpine areas (Leipzig), (various dates, pre-1939)
Baker, J. N. L. *History of Geographical Discovery and Exploration* (1931)
Bates, R. H. *Five Miles High* (1940)
Bauer, P. *Himalayan Campaign: The German Attack on Kangchenjunga* (1937)
——. *The Siege of Nanga Parbat 1856–1953* (1956)
Bechtold, F. *Nanga Parbat Adventure* (1935)
Bonington, C. *I Chose to Climb* (1966)
——. *Annapurna South Face* (1971)
——. *The Next Horizon* (1973)
Brown, J. *The Hard Years* (1967)
Brown, T. G. *Brenva* (1944)
Brown, T. G. and Beer, G. de. *The First Ascent of Mont Blanc* (1957)
Browne, B. *The Conquest of Mount McKinley* (Putnam, 1913)
Bruce, C. G. *The Assault on Mount Everest 1922* (1923)
Bryce, J. *Transcaucasia and Ararat* (4th ed, 1896)
Buehler, W. H. *Mountains of the World* (Vermont, 1970)
Buhl, H. *Nanga Parbat Pilgrimage* (1956)
Bury, C. K. Howard. *Mount Everest: The Reconnaissance, 1921* (1922)
Chevalley, G., Ditter, R., Lambert, R. *Avant-Premières à l'Everest*
Clark, R. *The Victorian Mountaineers* (1953)
——. *The Early Alpine Guides* (Phoenix, 1949)
Clark, R. W. and Pyatt, E. C. *Mountaineering in Britain* (Phoenix, 1957)
Collie, J. N. *Climbing on the Himalaya and Other Mountain Ranges* (1902)
Collomb, R. *Mountains of the Alps*
——. *Chamonix-Mount Blanc*
Conway, W. M. *Climbing and Exploration in the Karakoram Himalayas* (1894)
——. *Climbing and Exploration in the Bolivian Andes* (1901)
——. *Aconcagua and Tierra del Fuego* (1902)
Cook, F. A. *Bulletin of the American Geographical Society* (June, 1904)
——. *To the Top of the Continent* (1908)
Coolidge, W. A. B. Various works by this author (various dates)
Dyhrenfurth, G. O. *To the Third Pole* (Werner Laurie, 1955)
——. and Schneider. *Mount Everest* (1963)
Engel, C. E. *Mountaineering in the Alps* (rev ed, 1965)
Evans, C. *Kangchenjunga. The Untrodden Peak* (1956)
Filippi, Filippo de. *The Ascent of Mount St Elias* (1900)
——. *Karakoram and Western Himalaya 1909* (1912)
FitzGerald, E. A. *Climbs in the New Zealand Alps* (1896)
——. *The Highest Andes* (1899)
Forbes, J. D. *Travels Through the Alps of Savoy and Other Parts of the Pennine Chain* (1843)
Freshfield, D. W. *Travels in the Central Caucasus and Bashan* (1869)
——. *The Life of Horace-Bénédict de Saussure* (trs) (1920)

Gillman, P. and Haston, D. *Eiger Direct* (1966)
Girdlestone, A. G. *The High Alps Without Guides* (1870)
Green, W. S. *The High Alps of New Zealand* (1883)
——. *Among the Selkirk Glaciers* (1890)
Gribble, F. *The Early Mountaineers* (1899)
   Guida d'Italia, Touring Club Italiano. *Torino e Valle d'Aosta* (Milano, 1959)
Harper, A. *Pioneer Work in the Alps of New Zealand* (1896)
Harrer, H. *The White Spider* (rev edn, 1965)
Haston, D. *In High Places* (1972)
Herrligkoffer, K. M. *Nanga Parbat* (1954)
Herzog, M. *Annapurna* (1952)
Hornbein, T. F. *Everest: The West Ridge* (1966)
Houston, C. *K2: The Savage Mountain* (1955)
Humboldt, A. von. *Personal Narrative of Travels to the Equator Regions of the New Continent* (trs H. M. Williams) (1827)
Hunt, J. *The Ascent of Everest* (1953)
Jones, C. *Climbing in North America* (University of California Press, 1976)
Kain, C. *Where the Clouds Can Go* (ed. Thorington, J. M.) (New York, 1935)
Klucker, C. *Adventures of an Alpine Guide* (1932)
Longstaff, T. *This My Voyage* (1950)
Lunn, A. *A Century of Mountaineering* (1957)
Mason, K. *Abode of Snow* (1955)
   Mountain World Vols (Swiss Foundation for Alpine Research, 1953–69)
Mumm, A. L. *Five Months in the Himalaya* (1909)
Mummery, A. F. *My Climbs in the Alps and Caucasus* (1895)
Murray, W. H. *The Story of Everest* (1953)
Norton, E. F. *The Fight for Everest* (1925)
Noyce, W. *South Col* (1954)
Parrot, F. *Journey to Ararat* (1846, rep 1972)
Rébuffat, G. *Starlight and Storm* (1967)
——. *Men and the Matterhorn* (1967)
Rey, G. *The Matterhorn* (1907)
Ruttledge, H. *Everest 1933* (1934)
——. *Everest: The Unfinished Adventure* (1937)
Shackleton, E. *South* (1919)
Shipton, E. E. *Nanda Devi* (1936)
——. *Mountains of Tartary* (1951)
Smythe, F. S. *The Kangchenjunga Adventure* (1930)
——. *Kamet Conquered* (1932)
——. Camp 6 [1933 Everest Expedition] (1937)
——. *The Adventures of a Mountaineer* (1940)
Stephen, L. *The Playground of Europe* (1871)
Stutfield, H. E. and Collie, J. N. *Climbs and Exploration in the Canadian Rockies* (1903)
Tilman, H. W. *Ascent of Nanda Devi* (1937)
——. *Mount Everest 1938* (1948)
Tyndall, J. *Hours of Exercise in the Alps* (1871)
Ullman, J. R. *Americans on Everest* (1965)
——. Man of Everest (US *Tiger of the Snows*)—a life of Tenzing (1955)
——. and Murray, W. H. *The Age of Mountaineering* (1956)
Washburn, B. *A Tourist's Guide to Mt McKinley*
——. Essay in *Mountain World* 1956–7 on Mt McKinley (1957)
Whillans, D. *Portrait of a Mountaineer*
Whymper, E. *Scrambles Amongst the Alps in the Years 1860–9* (1871)
——. *Travels Amongst the Great Andes of the Equator* (1892)
Wills, A. *Wanderings Amongst the High Alps* (1856)
Younghusband, F. *The Heart of a Continent* (1896)
Zurbriggen, M. *From the Alps to the Andes* (1899)